THE THEOLOGY OF
TO THE ROMANS

Klaus Haacker, a respected expert on Paul's writings, presents a compelling introduction to the theology of the Letter to the Romans. This volume completes Cambridge's successful New Testament Theology series. In keeping with the series, it explores the distinctive ideas and issues of the Epistle at greater length than is possible in commentaries or theological dictionaries. Professor Haacker focuses on themes such as righteousness, suffering and hope, and the mystery of Israel in the age of the Gospel. Engaging with Paul's rhetoric strategy, he shows how both ancient Rome and the spiritual heritage of Israel provide contexts for the Letter and help us to understand its message to the original readers and its abiding impact on Christianity. The book will be of interest to teachers, pastors, and students of theology and the New Testament.

KLAUS HAACKER is Professor of New Testament Studies at the Barmen School of Theology, Wuppertal, Germany. He is the author of numerous scholarly publications on the Letter to the Romans and other Pauline texts, and has served as editor of the periodical *Theologische Beiträge* since 1977.

NEW TESTAMENT THEOLOGY

General editor: James D. G. Dunn,
Lightfoot Professor of Divinity, University of Durham

This series sets out to provide a programmatic survey of the individual writings of the New Testament. It aims to remedy the deficiency of available published material which concentrates on the New Testament writers' theological concerns. New Testament specialists here write at greater length than is usually possible in the introduction to commentaries or as part of other New Testament theologies, and explore the theological themes and issues of their chosen books without being tied to a commentary format, or to a thematic structure provided from elsewhere. Now complete, the series covers all the New Testament writings, and thus provides an attractive, and timely, range of texts around which courses can be developed.

All titles published in this series

THE THEOLOGY OF PAUL'S LETTER TO THE ROMANS

KLAUS HAACKER

Kirchliche Hochschule Wuppertal

CAMBRIDGE
UNIVERSITY PRESS

PUBLISHED BY THE PRESS SYNDICATE OF THE UNIVERSITY OF CAMBRIDGE
The Pitt Building, Trumpington Street, Cambridge, United Kingdom

CAMBRIDGE UNIVERSITY PRESS
The Edinburgh Building, Cambridge, CB2 2RU, UK
40 West 20th Street, New York, NY 10011–4211, USA
477 Williamstown Road, Port Melbourne, VIC 3207, Australia
Ruiz de Alarcón 13, 28014 Madrid, Spain
Dock House, The Waterfront, Cape Town 8001, South Africa

http://www.cambridge.org

© Klaus Haacker 2003

First published 2003

Printed in the United Kingdom at the University Press, Cambridge

Typeface Baskerville MT 11/12.5 pt.   *System* LaTeX 2$_\varepsilon$ [TB]

A catalogue record for this book is available from the British Library

Library of Congress Cataloging in Publication data
Haacker, Klaus.
The theology of Paul's letter to the Romans / Klaus Haacker.
p.   cm. – (New Testament theology)
Includes bibliographical references and index.
ISBN 0 521 43480 7 (hardback) – ISBN 0 521 43535 8 (paperback)
1. Bible. N.T. Romans – Theology.   I. Title.   II. Series.
BS2665.52H32   2003
227′.106 – dc21   2003046080

ISBN 0 521 43480 7 hardback
ISBN 0 521 43535 8 paperback

Contents

Abbreviations

ABR	Australian Biblical Review
AnBib	Analecta biblica
AncB	Anchor Bible
AugSt	Augustinian Studies
BJRL	Bulletin of the John Rylands Library
CBQ	Catholic Biblical Quarterly
CThM	Currrents in Theology and Mission
ET	Expository Times
HBT	Horizons in Biblical Theology
HTR	Harvard Theological Review
ICC	International Critical Commentary
Interp.	Interpretation
JJS	Journal of Jewish Studies
JRS	Journal of Roman Studies
JSNT.SS	Journal for the Study of the New Testament. Supplement series
JThSt	Journal of Theological Studies
NIC	New International Commentary
NT	Novum Testamentum
NTS	New Testament Studies
REAug	Revue des études augustiniennes
SNTS	Studiorum Novi Testamenti Societas
ThBeitr	Theologische Beiträge
ThHK	Theologischer Handkommentar
TynB	Tyndale Bulletin
TNTC	Tyndale New Testament Commentary
ZNW	Zeitschrift für die neutestamentliche Wissenschaft

CHAPTER I

Introduction

THEOLOGY OR LETTER — OR BOTH?

For centuries readers and expositors of Paul's Letter to the Romans took it for granted that this letter contained *theology*, i.e. Christian doctrine, more or less timeless truth about God and humankind presented in a consistent system of thought. This expectation left no room for doubts about statements which might have been relevant for a specific situation at the time of Paul and which could not be applied to very different situations of a later age. Therefore the Church fathers or the leaders of the Protestant Reformation could consult and appeal to the letter to the Romans as an answer to questions that were discussed among their contemporaries. This attitude changed gradually during the formative period of modern Bible study. As a first step, the Enlightenment introduced a distinction between eternal truth (defined as compatible with reason) and its accidental historical 'garments' (which could be neglected or disposed of by modern minds). The essential content of Scripture continued to be viewed as doctrine. But a door was opened for a closer look at circumstances and development. The next stage was the discovery of *different* theologies contained in different writings of the Old and New Testaments, reflections not only of changing times but also of personal profile. Sooner or later, this awareness of variety led to the question of relations and interactions between those different positions. Thus, partly under the auspices of Hegelian philosophy of history, the nineteenth century saw the emergence of the idea of early Christianity as a process of conflicting positions and movements. The quest for intentions began to prevail over mere expositions of content, and defining intentions implied research into the readers envisaged by particular writings. Biblical literature turned out to be the product of an interaction between writers and their public, just as any other literature. The easiest access to such interactions was provided by the genre of letters with their more or less reliable indications about sender and addressee. (It took much more time to understand that the gospels, too, are guided by needs of the public such as specific communities whom their authors wanted to influence.)

The twentieth century provided a widening of horizons for aspects of Biblical writings besides and beyond reading them as *theology*. Form criticism promoted an awareness of the community and its traditions as background and basis of religious writings. Existential philosophy prompted exegesis to ask for structures of human consciousness to be detected under the surface of texts, which, it was hoped, would facilitate their speaking to modern man. Later, in a more scientific vein, psychology and sociology were applied to the New Testament. Political commitments of our day have stimulated interest in the impact of the struggles of the century of the New Testament on the attitudes of early Christians. On the other hand, interpreters more deeply rooted in pastoral practice have discovered models for preaching or Church growth in various passages from the Acts of the Apostles and the New Testament letters.

Commentaries on Romans have shared this development and variety of approaches. To write a *theology* of Romans cannot mean to forget about our own place in the history of interpretation. Rather, we should widen our concept of *theology* so that it includes pastoral, social, political, and emotional dimensions. If theology centres on God, the creator of all, then it stands to reason that it should be holistic. And, after all, encountering Paul means facing a man of *passion* both before and after the famous turning point of his life connected with the city of Damascus. The letter to the Romans makes no exception – although it turns out to be the most elaborate, sometimes sophisticated, and in a way most mature of his extant writings.

WHOSE LETTER?

We are concerned with a letter of *Paul*. Which Paul? Of course, Paul the apostle, not to be confused with another Paul who is mentioned in Acts 13:7, a Roman governor of Cyprus. Unfortunately we do not know the full name of the apostle. As a Roman citizen (see Acts 16:37; 22:25–29; 23:27), he must have had a name consisting of at least three names, including the family name of that Roman leader who bestowed this citizenship on the Jewish family into which Paul was born.[1] In his writings he never uses this full name – thereby indicating that his civil status was of no importance for his sense of calling or his function in the early Church. (Nevertheless it must have facilitated contacts with higher classes and helped him to survive some conflicts during his missionary ministry.) In Romans there is a very faint hint of Paul's civic status: When in Rom. 13:6 he refers to the paying of tribute (not just 'taxes') as a symbol of submission to the Roman political order (including gratitude for its benefits) he does not say '*We* are paying tributes' but '*You* are paying tributes'. As a Roman citizen, Paul had to pay taxes from his trade but no tribute.

What is infinitely more important is Paul's *Jewish* origin and identity. He mentions it in Rom. 11:1; 2 Cor. 11:22; Phil. 3:5 and specifies it twice as descent from the patriarch Benjamin (see Rom. 11:1; Phil. 3:5), thus excluding suspicions (and later slanders) that he might be a proselyte and as such not really familiar with Jewish traditions. It fits well into this picture that Paul's Jewish name was Saul, no doubt chosen after the tragic, but in any case heroic, first king of Israel. This name was not replaced by 'Paul' after his conversion but continued to be used in Jewish circles (see Acts 7:58 – 13:9 *passim*). That Paul himself does not use this name when writing to mostly Gentile-Christians should not surprise us since the Greek word *saulos*, however rarely used, had a rather unfavourable meaning ('straddling' or 'waddling'). Luke, on the other hand, needed this Hebrew name of Paul in order to quote the words which Paul heard in his visionary experience near Damascus (see Acts 9:4; 22:7; 26:14) and which should remind readers of a scene from the conflict between David and Saul of old (see 1 Sam. 26:18). The name 'Paul' was very suitable for a diaspora Jew living in a Greek and Roman environment because in Latin it meant 'small' or 'little'.

In fact, Paul had been born in the town of Tarsus near the southern coast of Asia Minor (see Acts 21:39; 22:3). But in his letters he

---

[1] See Colin Hemer, 'The Name of Paul', *TynB* 36 (1985), 179–185.

never refers to this origin, and in Acts 22:3 Luke has him declare
that he had moved from Tarsus to Jerusalem at a very early age in
order to be brought up according to the Law under the supervi-
sion of Gamaliel the Elder, a famous Pharisee and expert of the
Law (see Acts 5:34). This passage leaves little if any space for
a deeper influence of a pagan surrounding on Paul during his
boyhood.[2] His command of the Greek language and such knowledge of Greek culture as can be detected in his letters can be easily
explained: (a) from educational facilities in Jerusalem itself; and
(b) from later periods of his life, including a longer stay at Tarsus
after his conversion (see Acts 9:30; 11:25). If Paul had been brought
up in Tarsus and significantly shaped by this cultural background,
he could hardly have called himself 'a Hebrew of Hebrews' in
Phil. 3:5.[3]

The association with Gamaliel the Elder mentioned in Acts 22:3
need not mean that Paul had entered 'theological studies' in order
to become a rabbi or sage. The words used in connection with
Gamaliel (*anatrepho* and *paideuo*) generally stand for education (a)
in the family; and (b) in school or school-like contexts, not for a
technical or professional training. If Gamaliel the Elder had been
a famous teacher of the Law (and Rabbinical sources confirm this
statement of Luke in Acts 5:34), that does not prevent him from
being in charge of the general religious education of boys from
upper-class Jewish families such as Paul's. Paul does not hesitate
to claim for himself any excellence that would be cherished by
contemporary Jews (see Phil. 3:4–6). But learning is not among the
things he is boasting of – neither here nor in Gal. 1:13–14, where
he insists on having been ahead of his fellows. It was his fervour
in militant activities, not intellectual prominence, which made him
'advance beyond' many of his Jewish contemporaries. So let us
forget about the 'rabbi' or 'extremely learned man' ('*vir doctissimus*',
as Jerome called Paul in his letter No. 120.11). Paul's knowledge
of Scripture was surely tremendous; but piety and religious zeal,

---

[2] See Willem Cornelis van Unnik, *Tarsus or Jerusalem: The City of Paul's Youth* (London, 1962);
pace some objections of Andrie B. du Toit, 'A Tale of Two Cities: "Tarsus or Jerusalem"
Revisited', *NTS* 46 (2000), 375–402.

[3] In Acts 6:1 'Hebrews' is the opposite of 'Hellenists', the latter being Jews with Greek
names.

together with intellectual ability and higher education, are enough to account for Paul's familiarity with the Old Testament and for his skill in its application to controversial topics of early Christian discussions.

A self-designation not easily reconciled with the older assumption of a Hellenistic background is Paul's claim in Phil. 3:5 to have been a *Pharisee*. In his lifetime this was the most influential party of Judaism – in the Jewish homeland. There are virtually no traces of Pharisaism in Jewish communities of the diaspora. In the eyes of many specialists in Pauline studies, this Pharisaic background is the decisive clue to his Jewish identity 'before Damascus' and to his radical re-evaluation of Jewish values (especially the Law) 'after Damascus'. This widespread assurance stands in sharp contrast to the fact that we have so little reliable knowledge about the doctrines of the Pharisees of Paul's day. We can be sure about their vital interest in an interpretation of the Law that was flexible enough to meet the requirements of everyday life in circumstances that differed much from Old Testament times. By the time of Jesus's public ministry, these efforts had already produced a time-honoured tradition (*paradosis*) that was ascribed to the 'fathers', i.e., former generations of teachers. The discussion about purity in Mark 7 reflects tensions between this tradition and a literal interpretation and application of the Law (one of the rare points of contact between Jesus and the Sadducees against the Pharisees). In the course of time, this tradition developed into collections such as the Mishnah (*c.* AD 200) and the two Talmudim (fifth–seventh centuries AD). While some continuity between the Pharisees and these Rabbinical collections is as a rule assumed, the historical value of this literature as evidence for the first century AD has been questioned by many specialists.[4]

On the other hand, the way in which Pharisees are depicted in the New Testament is held to be distorted by the conflicts between early Christian communities and their Jewish counterparts and rivals. That leaves us very much dependent on the relevant passages in the writings of Josephus, who confesses to have joined

[4] See e.g., Jacob Neusner, *The Rabbinic Traditions about the Pharisees before 70* (Leiden: Brill 1971), 3 vols.; *Judaism in the Beginning of Christianity* (Philadelphia: Fortress Press, 1984), ch. 3.

the Pharisees as a young man (see *Life* 12). However, the fact that
he connects this step with his starting out on a political career has –
together with other observations – created serious doubts concerning the genuineness of his Pharisaic allegiance.[5] Apart from this,
his reports on Pharisaic doctrine in comparison with other groups
of early Judaism are coloured by his use of Greek philosophical
terminology (such as *fate* or *destiny* or *immortality*) instead of faithful
quotations from genuine Jewish sources. Despite these problems, it
is fairly certain that the Pharisees where keen on modelling their
lives according to the Law because they expected a final judgement on each individual, resulting in eternal life or eternal doom.
The focus of this understanding of human existence and the aim of
one's efforts to live up to God's standards was the idea of *righteousness*
(not in the Greek sense of treating others justly, but in the sense of
being right in God's sight); see Matt. 5:20; Luke 18:9. Paul shared
this concern as a Pharisee, but was compelled to a new and different solution by his encounter with the Risen Lord (cf. Phil. 3:5–6
with 7–9). Large parts of his letters to the Galatians and to the
Romans reflect this change of mind, and try to bring it home to
fellow-Christians who were reluctant to draw the far-reaching
consequences which Paul had drawn and proclaimed.[6]

How much do we learn by knowing that Paul was a Pharisee?
What does this background contribute to our understanding of his
personal profile or his peculiar stance within Judaism and early
Christianity? Not really much, for to be a Pharisee in his lifetime
meant little more than to be a member of a mainstream religious
movement. But obviously Paul was more than just an ordinary Jew
of his time (and an ordinary Christian after his conversion). We
know for certain that he was a man of conflict and controversy.
So we must go on to ask what made him stand out from his social
context. To all who can read he is quite clear about this question. In
Gal. 1:14 he writes: 'I was advancing in Judaism beyond many Jews
of my own age and was extremely zealous for the traditions of my
fathers.' With this sentence Paul explains why he had persecuted the

[5] See Steve Mason, 'Was Josephus a Pharisee? A Re-Examination of Life 10–12', *JJS* 40
(1989), 31–45.
[6] See below, ch. 4.

Church so violently and had tried to destroy it (v. 13). It is here that we can feel the very heartbeat of the 'early' Paul, his very special sense of calling in terms of his Jewish tradition. For the fact that Paul had persecuted the Jesus movement is one of the best-attested facts of New Testament history; at least it is the information about Paul's youth that surpasses all others in frequency (see Acts 7:58; 8:1; 9:1 s, 5, 13–14, 21; 22:4–5, 7, 19; 26:9–11, 14; 1 Cor. 15:9; Gal. 1:13, 23; Phil. 3:6; 1 Tim. 1:13).[7]

As for the motives behind this activity, the conjunction of 'zeal' and 'persecution' rings a bell that recurs in other statements about Paul's past both in his own letters (see Phil. 3:6) and in the Acts of the Apostles (see Acts 22:3–4), and which reminds us of a long range of Biblical examples such as Phineas (see Num. 25:6–13; Ps. 106:30–31; Sir. 45:28–32; 1 Macc. 2:26,54; 4 Macc. 18:12), Saul (see 1 Sam. 28:9); Elijah (see 1 Kgs. 18:40; 19:14), and Jehu (see 2 Kgs. 10:16). All of them fought against apostasy from Israel's God and similar temptations. Their strategy was to kill individuals who had introduced pagan practices in order to save the whole people from an impending wrath (or 'zeal') of God (thereby being 'zealous' for, and on behalf of, God). Their example inspired the resistance of the Maccabees against the attempt of a thorough-going religious Hellenisation of Judaea in the second century BCE and at least parts of the groups that conspired against the Romans during Paul's lifetime, and led the people into rebellion shortly after his death.[8] These movements in early Judaism are misunderstood if we interpret them on a merely secular line of modern concepts of national independence. Their motivation was clearly religious, and they implied a large measure of civil war against compatriots who deviated from what was considered to be vital for Israel's future as dependent upon God's favour. When Paul reminds his readers of his former violence against 'the church of God' and of the religious reasons

---

[7] The historical question whether all the measures Paul is said to have taken against the followers of Jesus fit into the context of legal and political conditions of his time cannot be discussed here. We must reckon with the possibility of exaggeration, but also with a tendency to make certain actions appear legal when in reality they were not.

[8] See William R. Farmer, *Maccabees, Zealots, and Josephus. An Inquiry into Jewish Nationalism in the Greco-Roman Period* (New York, 1956); Martin Hengel, *The Zealots: Investigation into the Jewish Freedom Movement in the Period from Herod until AD 70* (Edinburgh: Clark, 1969).

behind it, he confesses to have shared this tradition.[9] In his sight, the Jesus movement must have looked like a syncretistic development within Israel which – if not suppressed – could call God's wrath on the people as a whole.[10]

This biographical background is important for understanding the dynamics of his personal development and the vigour of some of his later convictions and controversies. To give just one example: while Paul's attitude towards the non-Jewish world was radically changed, his passionate allegiance to his people was in no wise weakened (as will be discussed in chapter 4). Above all, his very notion of the essence of Judaism must have grown up with him during the formative years of his life. After all, he had striven to live Jewish identity at its best.[11] And since this attitude had caused him to oppose the Jesus movement, his own former outlook serves as a model when in his letters he is talking about the Jews who do not respond to the Christian message.

All this information on the early life of Paul cannot explain the heart of his theology. It describes the ingredients but says little about the cake. The essential source of or *the key to the theology of Paul*[12] is his experience on the road to Damascus, where the persecutor was transformed into a preacher of what he had sought to suppress.[13] He speaks of it as a *revelation* given to him by God concerning his son Jesus Christ, and denies any human influence on the core of his preaching (see Gal. 1:11–12,16). Does this rule out any attempt to understand the making of his theology on the basis of his personal development? Far from it: it is just in this context that Paul makes those statements about his past which we have made use of already. The 'Damascus event' was a real *encounter* of two parties – one

---

[9] See e.g., Mark R. Fairchild, 'Paul's Pre-Christian Zealot Associations: A Re-Examination of Gal. 1:14 and Acts 22:3', *NTS* 45 (1999), 514–532.

[10] The reasons for this view are not easy to detect. They cannot have been matters of mere doctrine (including Christology). Maybe Paul regarded the miracles performed by Jesus and the apostles as acts of magic (see Mark 3:22; Acts 4:7; 5:12–18).

[11] The term *ioudaïsmos* in Gal. 1:13 does not simply mean 'Judaism' but something like 'Jewish endeavour' or *commitment to* (a purer or better) Judaism.

[12] That was the title of a fine little book in German by Joachim Jeremias published in 1971 which made this point.

[13] See Gal. 1:23, the shortest summary of this event, quoting the news that spread in the congregations of Judea: 'The man who formerly persecuted us is now preaching the faith he once tried to destroy.'

on earth and one in heaven – and as such it had such powerful consequences. And, if we can believe Luke, this event implied an encounter of Paul not only with Christ but also with himself when the Risen Lord calls him by his name (his *Jewish* name *Saul*) and questions his eager activities: 'Why do you persecute me?' (see Acts 9:5; 22:7; 26:14). In mathematical terms, the peculiar theology of Paul is the 'resultant' out of the 'horizontal' force of his previous life and the 'vertical' force of divine intervention.

Can we *know* anything for certain about such supernatural experiences? Nothing, if by 'knowing' we mean more than to describe human experience. But if we content ourselves with that, our sources do reveal several aspects of this turning point in Paul's life:

1. It was an encounter with the Risen Jesus comparable with the experiences of the disciples recorded in the final chapters of the Gospels (see 1 Cor. 9:1; 15:8). Apparently it made no difference to Paul (if we can believe Luke's report in Acts) that he had not 'seen' Jesus in the same way as the disciples but only heard His voice speaking from heaven. In any case the effect of the event was his 'knowledge of Christ Jesus' as his Lord (see Phil. 3:8).

2. In the light of numerous stories of persecutors who finally met disaster as they deserved,[14] Paul should have expected sudden punishment when he learned that the disciples whom he had despised and hunted were right in their belief in the resurrection of this Jesus of Nazareth. Obviously he was spared and even called to a mission he did not deserve; so 'grace' became a hallmark of the lesson he learned in Damascus (see 1 Cor. 15:8–9).

3. In recent years there has been a vivid discussion about whether the Damascus event should be labelled Paul's 'conversion' or whether we should prefer the term 'calling'.[15] There are some connotations of the term 'conversion' that cannot and should not be applied to the biography of Paul: the notion of turning from one religion to another, or assumptions about what a genuine Christian

---

[14] Paul's older contemporary Philo wrote such a story in his book *Against Flaccus* (a Roman prefect of Egypt who had treated the Jews brutally and was finally sentenced to death under Caligula).

[15] See Krister Stendahl, *Paul Among Jews and Gentiles and Other Essays* (Philadelphia: Fortress Press, 1976).

conversion should look like – starting with despair of oneself and
a yearning for salvation.[16] But these are unnecessarily narrow definitions of 'conversion' which are not binding on our usage of the
term. If we leave all prejudice aside, we arrive at the balanced view
that some texts about the 'Damascus event' contain nothing or little on the line of 'calling' but justify the heading 'conversion' (see
Phil. 3:4–11; Acts 9:1–18), while others concentrate on the 'calling'
aspect (see 1 Cor. 9:1; 15:8–11; Gal. 1:11–23; Acts 22:3–16 (with
its continuation in v. 17–21 concerning Paul's being sent to the
Gentiles); 26:4–20 (strengthening the 'calling' aspect by words of
the Risen Lord not paralleled in ch. 9 and 22)). A rather balanced
blending of both aspects is found in 1 Tim. 1:12–16, enriched with
categories of a moral interpretation of Paul's conversion that prepared the way for reading it as a model (in fact as *the* paradigm) of
sinners finding forgiveness from God's mercy.

   4. What is clear beyond doubt is that Paul dates his status as
'apostle' back to this event (see 1 Cor. 9:1; 15:8; Gal. 11:11–17) and
that he does so because others questioned or opposed this claim of
his. The sense of calling that was condensed in this title contributes
much to the character of Paul's Letter to the Romans.[17]

   As for influences on Paul *after* his conversion/call, there is little
evidence and therefore much room for guesswork. He must have
learned something from the congregation at Damascus where he
was baptised and immediately started to testify to his new belief in
Jesus Christ (see Acts 9:10–22; 22:12–16). He seems to have paid a
rather short visit to Jerusalem about two years later (see Gal. 1:18;
Acts 9:26–30) followed by a stay of unknown length and unknown
activities at Tarsus. From there Barnabas called him to join the
flourishing congregation of Antioch in Syria (see Acts 11:25s), which
in time became the basis of the first venture to spread Christianity
by travelling missionaries (Barnabas and Paul; see Acts 13–14). By
that time Antioch (the biggest city of the empire after Rome and
Alexandria) had become an important centre of early Christianity,
founded by fugitives from among the Hellenists of Jerusalem (see
Acts 8:1, 11:19). According to Acts 11:19–20 some of them (by no

[16] Take, e.g., the beginning of John Bunyan's *Pilgrim's Progress*, first published in 1678.
[17] See below, in ch. 2.

means all) decided to preach the Gospel not only to Jews but also to 'Greeks' or 'Hellenists',[18] and that caused a controversy between them and conservative Jewish Christians from Judea (see Acts 15; Gal. 2:1–10). In the course of these discussions Paul became increasingly aware of his duty to *defend* this widening of the horizon towards a world-wide mission of the Church – one of the major topics of Romans (as of Galatians before).

Luke's notice that it was then and there that the followers of Jesus were called 'Christians' for the first time calls for attention. Since *christianos* is a Latin word (apart from the Greek ending '*os*') meaning 'adherents or partisans of a man named Christ', it presupposes that the Roman authorities began to be interested in the Jesus movement. The term certainly does *not* prove (as some have proposed) that it was in Antioch by that early date that Christianity had become a religion to be distinguished from Judaism. We may trace this view to Antioch – but only at a much later date, in the letters of Ignatius of Antioch.[19] Paul's Letter to the Romans contains a quite different lesson to be learned on the relationship between the faith of Israel and belief in Jesus Christ.

TO WHOM?

The name of our letter 'To the Romans' is in a sense misleading because in the first century it would have meant 'To Roman citizens' excluding foreigners (*peregrini*) who merely lived in the capital. In reality, Paul writes this letter to 'people living in Rome' (1:7,15)[20] who, as mere subjects of the Roman nation, had to pay tributes (see 13:6). Less than ten years after the writing of this letter many of them would be crucified – a punishment from which citizens were exempt.[21] That the addressees are Christians is clear from the beginning because Paul introduces them already in v. 6 as 'called by Jesus Christ' – a remarkable definition of their identity by a task

---

[18] Manuscripts are divided in this place and the original reading is uncertain.

[19] See Ign. Magn. 10:3.

[20] The variant readings without 'in Rome' in both verses are poorly attested and can be neglected.

[21] See Tacitus, *Annals* 15:44; and Peter Lampe, *Die stadtrömischen Christen in den ersten beiden Jahrhunderten. Untersuchungen zur Sozialgeschichte* (Tübingen: Mohr-Siebeck, 1989), 66.

or vocation, not by belief. But that follows in v. 8. Some have missed the term 'church' in this address and inferred that for Paul these Christians in Rome did not yet deserve the appellation 'church' because they still waited for an apostolic blessing. But that sounds anachronistic. The term 'church' is lacking also in the address of the Letter to the Philippians – Paul's 'favourite congregation' (see Phil. 4:15–16). As yet, the deeper meaning of these two exceptions has escaped our knowledge.

But what can be known about the first readers of Romans (or better 'listeners', when the letter was read in their meetings)? We may know quite a number of their names – if chapter 16, with its many greetings, was part of the original letter. For several reasons this assumption has been questioned, but the arguments against its authenticity are not compelling.[22] So we can learn from this chapter that the readers consisted of several groups, mainly house churches, who seem to have met in different quarters of the capital – too numerous or too distant from each other to form one congregation. Also too different from each other? In the light of chapters 14 and 15:1–7 this question may well be asked.[23]

It is generally agreed that most of the Roman Christians were Gentiles. However, not all statements of Paul say that clearly. According to 1:5–6 the addressees are 'among', not 'from' the nations or Gentiles. In 11:13 the phrase 'I am talking to you Gentiles' could mean: 'The following argument (as distinct from the letter as such) is directed to you Gentiles.' But in 1:13 'among you as among the other Gentiles' is strong evidence. That does not mean that Paul is speaking only to a Gentile audience; in 2:17 he explicitly addresses a Jewish interlocutor (though only rhetorically). But for the intention of Romans it is important so see that Gentile Christians are Paul's primary partners in the letter itself and in his plans for the future (see 1:11–15; 15:14–29).

That Jewish Christians (or Christian Jews) probably were a minority is usually seen as a result of conflicts in the late forties which led to an expulsion of Jews from the capital, mentioned in Acts 18:2 and by Suetonius in his *Life of Claudius* (25:4). Many scholars are

[22] See especially H. Gamble Jr, *The Textual History of the Letter to the Romans. A Study in Textual and Literary Criticism* (Grand Rapids, 1977); and P. Lampe, *Die stadtrömischen Christen*, 124–135.
[23] See below, ch. 4.

convinced that the name *Chrestus*, denoting the instigator of public riots in the passage of Suetonius, is a misspelling of *Christus*. That in turn leads to the assumption that the Roman authorities held a group of *Christiani* (= followers of Christ) responsible for this civic unrest. Judging from the evidence of Acts concerning local conflicts in, and with, Jewish congregations confronted with the Christian message, it is more than likely that the beginnings of Christianity in Rome were as early as some time before Paul's arrival at Corinth, i. e. before AD 50.[24]

The size of this expulsion of Jews from Rome cannot easily be estimated. Luke's witness in Acts 18:2 allows the idea that there were tens of thousands of Jews affected by the edict of Claudius who were forced to leave the city (among them the Christian couple Aquila and Priscilla mentioned by Luke). But his speaking of 'all' Jews is not confirmed by Suetonius, whose '*Iudaeos*' might even be reduced to mean only 'some Jews' because in Latin there is no definite article. However, the context of this short notice mentions other measures of the emperor against several groups of people as a whole (including ethnic groups). Therefore we should be on safe ground to assume that at least all Jewish inhabitants of Rome who did not possess the Roman citizenship lost their residence permit. For many of them it must have been a heavy blow, and if the appearance of Christian groups in Roman synagogues had triggered this conflict, serious repercussions on the witness to Jews may have followed.

By the time Paul is writing his letter, the legal situation should have changed (with the edict of Claudius having expired with the emperor's death in October 54). Like other Jews, Jewish Christians would have returned to the capital, among them Aquila and Priscilla (see Rom. 16:3). But memories of the disaster must have remained and may have resulted in a more cautious way of presenting the Christian message to local Jews and in an increased consideration of possible political pressure.

When we compare Paul's initial thanksgiving for the spiritual situation of the addressees in 1:8 with other letters, we can hardly

---

[24] See Colin Hemer, 'Observations on Pauline Chronology', in *Pauline Studies. Essays Presented to Professor F. F. Bruce on his 70th Birthday*, ed. D. A. Hagner and M. J. Harris (Exeter and Grand Rapids, 1980), 3–18, esp. 8.

escape the observation that it sounds 'exceptionally brief and formal'.[25] To say that 'your faith is being reported all over the world' means nothing more than that the news of a Christian community in Rome has spread to a general public[26] as far as the provinces – perhaps an allusion to the crisis under Claudius. From a distance, Paul could have given it a positive interpretation (see Phil. 1:12–14, 18). To find another (and fuller) praise of the addressees we must read on to chapter 15:14, and this one, too, is rather short and again serves to prelude statements of Paul on himself and his plans, just as in chapters 1:9–15. It cannot be ruled out that the tensions discussed in chapter 14 somehow tainted the image of the Roman Christians in the eyes of the apostle. On the other hand, according to 1:12 he hopes to be encouraged himself while sharing his faith with the Romans. Unfortunately we have no further information, but whatever this means, we observe a striking disproportion between what Paul is affirming about himself and his laconic comment on the faith of the Romans, if compared with the praise that others receive.

WHEN AND WHY?

We are on much firmer ground concerning the situation in Paul's life at the time when he wrote this letter. Although there is some uncertainty concerning the exact year (AD 56 or 57), there can be no doubt as to the place of Romans in the course of events of Paul's life: According to Rom. 15:25–27 Paul wrote this letter just before a journey to Jerusalem, where he intended to deliver the money collected by Gentile congregations for the poorer believers in Judea. From Acts 20:1–6 we learn that during the months before that journey Paul stayed in Greece and Macedonia. A certain Gaius, whose hospitality is praised in Rom. 16:23, could be the one mentioned in 1 Cor. 1:14, and the mentioning of Phoebe in Rom. 16:1 as being in the service of the congregation at Cenchrea (the eastern port of Corinth) also supports the assumption of a Corinthian origin of

---

[25] L. A. Jervis, *The Purpose of Romans. A Comparative Letter Structure Investigation* (Sheffield: JSOT, 1991). p. 107.
[26] See 1 Thess. 1:8.

the letter. In fact this lady seems to have been entrusted with the delivery of the letter to Rome (see v. 2).

If the apostle did write the Letter to the Romans at this point of his life we must keep in mind the importance of this collection in the eyes of Paul – and the risks he took in connection with it. A financial relief for the mother church of Jerusalem had been organised for the first time by the congregation of Antioch in Syria, and Barnabas and Paul had travelled to Jerusalem for this purpose (see Acts 11:27–30; 12:25). Their second visit to Jerusalem as representatives of Antioch was prompted by the controversy about the demand of a Jewish–Christian pressure group that Gentile Christians had to be circumcised (see Acts. 15:1–5).[27] This conflict was settled by the so-called Apostolic Council with a decision against this programme which had implied a reduction of the Christian mission to a variant of Early Jewish proselytism. According to Gal. 2:1–10, the meeting resulted in another agreement: Paul and his colleagues should continue to evangelise among Gentiles while Peter was formally confirmed as in charge of the mission to the Jews. The only exception to this division of their mission fields was that Antioch should continue to support the poorer Christians in Judea (see Gal. 2:6–10).[28] Seen in this context, Paul's journey to Jerusalem had a highly symbolic meaning as an expression of the unity of the Church and of the acceptance of Gentile communities as equal partners of the original Church of Judea. This is one of the reasons why Paul had been busy with 'fund-raising' among his congregations for several years.[29]

With this background in mind, it sounds rather alarming when Paul, in Rom. 15:30–31, urges the Roman believers 'to join me in my struggle by praying to God for me' not only 'that I may be

[margin notes: 1st visit to Rome · financial relief · 2nd visit to Rome · J-Xian conflict]

---

[27] In view of chronological problems (see Gal. 1.18; 2:1) some scholars suggest that the two journeys of Luke's report in reality were one and the same, only remembered under two different aspects.

[28] The *monon* here in v. 10 introduces an exception to the agreement mentioned in v. 9 and not (as is all too often assumed) an exception to the statement of v. 6 (taken to speak of no additional obligations put on Paul and his converts).

[29] Rom. 15:27 interprets it on a different line – as an act of gratitude of Gentile Christians for the spiritual blessings which they had received from the original Church of Judea. In 2 Cor. 8–9 Paul offers various other reasons for generous contributions to this relief. No doubt his own determination to organise this collection and to complete it in person is the consequence of its being part and parcel of the agreement at the 'Jerusalem council'.

rescued from the unbelievers in Judea' but also 'that my service in Jerusalem may be acceptable to the saints there'. In other words, on the eve of his departure for Jerusalem, Paul was by no means certain that the Jewish Christians would welcome the gifts of the churches Paul had planted. Obviously, times had been changing and the harmony which Paul recalls in Gal. 2:1–10 could no longer be taken for granted.

It is generally agreed that by the time Paul is writing this letter, his position in the East had been weakened. Already Gal. 2:11–14 speaks of a backlash some time after the 'Apostolic Council' when Paul stood alone to defend table fellowship between Jewish and Gentile Christians at Antioch. The report in Acts 21 on Paul's arrival in Jerusalem spells out beyond doubt how justified the apostle's apprehensions had been: at the welcome meeting of Paul and his company with representatives of the local church, he first gives an account on 'what God had done among the Gentiles through his ministry' (Acts 21:19). In response, the apostle is informed of a questionable development in Judea. In number, there has been a remarkable church growth: 'Many thousands of Jews have become believers.' But (how alarming to Paul, who knew what this meant!): 'All of them are zealous for the law' (v. 20). As such, they are all too ready to believe rumours spread about Paul as teaching apostasy among the Jews of the diaspora (v. 21).

As for the collection (Paul's main reason for this dangerous journey for which he had postponed his missionary plans in the West), we can only guess whether it was accepted or not. When writing Rom. 15:31 Paul may have known already (what we learn from Josephus) that in these years there was a discussion in Judea about whether or not it was lawful to accept gifts from Gentiles. Eventually, in AD 66, the priests in power decided to refuse the financial support for their temple service which the Romans had granted for many years (as other pagan overlords before).[30] For this ideology of segregation there will have been no difference between the grants of a pagan ruler and the gifts of uncircumcised Gentile Christians. The message contained in Paul's collection must have been against the grain of these hardliners in Judea, and apparently many Jewish Christians sympathised strongly with this mentality.

[30] See Josephus, *Bell.* 2: 408–9.

Paul seems to have been conscious of his negative image that is attested in Acts 21:21. In Rom. 3:8 he quotes a slogan that has been put into his mouth by slanderers: 'Let us do evil that good may result!' This saying (which he disclaims scornfully) betrays the difficulties of law-abiding Jewish Christians with daring sentences of Paul such as Rom. 5:20: 'The law was added so that the trespass might increase. But where sin increased, grace increased all the more.'[31] Obviously the opposition he eventually met in Jerusalem was already filling his mind when he wrote the Letter to the Romans. The pains he took to clarify his understanding of the Law (especially in Rom. 7) and his attitude towards Israel (see Rom. 9–11) may be a tribute to discussions he had triggered with his Letter to the Galatians and which he expects during his visit to Judea. That is the truth behind the provocative formula of Ernst Fuchs and Jacob Jervell that the Letter to the Romans was also a 'letter to Jerusalem' (in a deeper sense, not to question the address given in Rom. 1:7,15).[32]

All this information on the critical point in Paul's life at the time of the composition of Romans should not distract us from the perspective which the apostle opens in the introduction to his letter in Rom. 1:8–17. After all, it is here that we find the background which he wanted the original readers to have in mind when reading the body of the letter. The clues we get from Rom. 15 are important for a deeper understanding of the mind of Paul, but if we let the author himself lead us into his writing we must realise that he wanted this letter to be read within a *missionary perspective*, primarily as a preparation for, and a foretaste of, a visit to Rome and a ministry there (see Rom. 1:9–15). In this opening passage of the letter, Paul uses rather strong terms to assure the readers of his long-standing wish and even several definite plans to come to Rome (vv. 10–13). His allusion to obstacles which prevented him from realising these plans (v. 13) may refer to consequences of the expulsion of Jews under Claudius, of which Paul heard through Aquila and Priscilla at Corinth (see Acts 18:2), if not already at Thessalonica. There he had been confronted with political accusations against his evangelism

---

[31] Although this idea is not found explicitly in earlier letters of Paul, Gal. 3:19 (the Law 'was added because of transgressions') could and can be understood on this line.

[32] See Jacob Jervell, 'The Letter to Jerusalem', in *The Romans Debate. Revised and Expanded Edition*, ed. Karl P. Donfried Peabody, Mass.: Hendrickson, 1991), 53–64.

and decided not to continue his journey westward on the *via Egnatia*, but turned south towards Athens and Corinth (see Acts 17:6–7, 10–15). Having stated his general commission to evangelise among non-Jews in Rom. 1:5, he goes on in v. 14 to emphasise that this meant an obligation to cross the borders between different nationalities and the barriers between cultural levels of society– sufficient reason for his eagerness to add the capital to the series of cities where he had preached in the years before. There was no place on earth where the universalism of Paul's sense of calling could be put in practice more directly than in Rome, where people from all parts of the empire and from all cultural backgrounds met and mingled.

On the other hand, Paul hesitated to intrude into a congregation which had not been founded by him (see Rom. 15:20) and which had not invited him to join its ministry (as did Antioch according to Acts 11:25–26). At least one of 'the reasons for Romans' (Wedderburn) must therefore have been to introduce himself to the believers in Rome in order to pave his way and to test their readiness to receive him and to co-operate with him.

When the readers come to near the end of the letter, they learn that Rome is not meant to become Paul's final residence but only a stop on his way to Spain (15:24, 28). There may be a double message in these remarks. For those who might be afraid of, or hostile to, a prolonged stay and a too-powerful influence of the apostle, this limitation of his visit could play down its importance. On the other hand, for those who would welcome him wholeheartedly and who were ready to assist and support him, this information had the quality of a request: what do you think of my plans? Could you contribute to this new outreach towards the 'ends of the earth' (see Isa. 49:6 as quoted by Paul in Acts 13:47)?[33]

For some recent authors on Romans such as *Peter Stuhlmacher*,[34] this 'Spanish perspective' is the apostle's decisive reason for writing Romans. They can rightly refer to Rom. 15:20–21 where Paul stresses that it is his ambition to work as a missionary pioneer

---

[33] For a discussion of Paul's 'theological geography', see R. Riesner, *Paul's Early Period* (1998), § 13.2: Geographic framework of the mission, 241–256.

[34] See his chapter, 'The Purpose of Romans', in *The Romans Debate. Revised and Expanded Edition* (1991), 231–242; and his commentary, *Der Brief an die Römer*, ed. Karl P. Donfried (Göttingen / Zürich, 1989), 211–212.

in regions hitherto unreached by the Gospel. But his real practice seems to have been different; otherwise he would not have
chosen Ephesus as one of his strongholds for quite a long time. The
theoretical principle of non-interference in existing congregations
and the announcement of missionary plans for Spain are closely
interwoven with expressions of Paul's strong desire to enjoy the fellowship of the Roman Christians as soon as possible (see vv. 23–24,
2.29:32, taking up the line of 1:9–14). We get the impression that –
under the cover of preparing for his outreach to Spain – Paul would
not have resented a rather long stay at Rome, comparable with his
earlier stays at Corinth or Ephesus. The apostle seems to be open to
both developments, depending on the reactions in Rome to his epistle and on his reception there in due time. In any case, Stuhlmacher
is right in assuming that in writing Romans Paul makes every effort to pave his way to Rome and to dispel all doubts about the
validity of his message which his opponents had disseminated (see
Rom. 3:8). Some of his readers may have been content with his
appeal to his authority (see 1:1–6; 11:13; 15:15–16) and obvious
success (see 15:17–19). Others will have been impressed by his argument from Scripture (see chapters 3–4, 9–11, 15) or from human
experience (see chapters 2:14–15; 7:7–25). Still others may have
been won by the local influence of those members of the Christian
groups in Rome whom Paul mentions with praise in the greetings of
chapter 16.

There seems to have been only one major obstacle to Paul's
plans in and with Rome: according to Rom. 14 there must have
been serious tensions within or between the local groups of believers. They are discussed by Paul at considerable length and with
great caution. The support by only one faction of Christianity in
Rome would not have served the purposes which Paul had in mind.
Apart from this, the very thought of a local Church divided into
conflicting parties was a horror to the apostle (see Rom. 16:17–20).
In 1 Corinthians he had fought against the formation of 'fan clubs'
of different teachers or preachers at Corinth (see 1 Cor. 1–4), and
in all probability Corinth is the place where Paul wrote the Letter
to the Romans. The warning in Rom. 16:17 sounds as if the mere
fact of divisions was more dangerous in the eyes of Paul than the
(possibly doctrinal) reasons which might have caused them.

It is clear beyond doubt that harmony within the Church (locally as universally) ranges among the major concerns of Paul. But this aspect should not be overestimated; it can in no wise account for the whole richness and depth of Paul's argument in this letter. Therefore the proposals to regard Rom. 14 as the very climax of, and clue to, this letter[35] should be dismissed as exaggerations. While at first sight it sounds reasonable that the *practical* aims of a letter of Paul's should be sought in its *ethical* passages (e.g., in Rom. 12:1–15:13[36]), we must keep in mind that Paul's activity as a missionary is the primary 'practice' into which all his letter-writing is embedded and which it is meant to serve. His pastoral comments on local problems of Rome (cautiously labelled as 'bold' in 15:15) are only one part of his strategy to set the stage for his intended entrance on the scene of the capital of the empire, officially regarded as the centre of the inhabited world (see Luke 2:1). With the 'troubles' under Claudius in mind, reflections on the relationship between (Jewish) Christians and (other) Jews, between Jews and Gentiles at large and between conflicting movements within early Christianity were a 'must' in the context of the ambitious vision of Paul's mission to the West. To sum it up in one sentence: the character and purpose of this letter result from *who* Paul had become as an individual and *what* he believed was his commission, *when* in his life he wrote this letter and *where* he intended to go (Jerusalem – Rome – Spain).

---

35 See Paul S. Minear, *The Obedience of Faith. The Purposes of Paul in the Epistle to the Romans* (London, 1971).

36 Similarly Neil Elliott, *The Rhetoric of Romans. Argumentative Constraint and Strategy and Paul's Dialogue with Judaism* (Sheffield, 1990), finds its climax in the ethical impact of Rom. 11:17–24.

CHAPTER 2

Theology in a nutshell: The opening of the letter as a foretaste of what follows

For didactic reasons the opening formula of Romans offers itself as an entrance into the theology of the letter. These seven verses are easy to memorise and can serve as a helpful frame for keeping important topics or aspects of Romans in mind.

All letter openings of Paul share a structure of three parts: sender, addressee, greeting. In some cases the opening contains little more than the names of persons and places (see 1 Thess. 1:1; Phil. 1:1–2). In others we find substantial extensions of certain parts (e.g., of the address in 1 Cor. 1:2 or of the greeting in Gal. 1:3–5). These extensions are no mere embellishments but a deliberate, premeditated prospectus of the following letter.[1] Thus in Gal. 1:1 the double 'no' 'apostle not of human origin nor through human mediation' anticipates Gal 1:10–24, where Paul insists on his independence from Jerusalem because of his being called by a direct revelation from God. His mentioning of Christ's death in Gal.1:4 interprets the term 'grace' of the greeting in v. 3 in a way which recurs in Gal. 2:20–21. The address of Galatians is the shortest of all: apparently Paul had no mind to pay compliments to the Galatian churches: they were still churches, of course, but . . . (see Gal. 1:6–8).

In the light of these examples, it cannot be by chance that the opening of Romans is by far the longest of all Pauline letters. What makes it so long? The greeting in 1:7b is identical with almost all counterparts in the other letters (only 1 Thess. 1:1 is shorter). The address in 1:7a says little more than that the letter is to be sent to Christians at Rome. All the rest – 1:1–6 – is an expansion of

---

[1] See L. Ann Jervis, *The Purpose of Romans. A Comparative Letter Structure Investigation,* JSNT.SS 55 (Sheffield, 1991).

the name of the sender (who in this case is Paul alone, while in all other letters Paul associates himself with others!). Already this rather formal observation justifies the expectation that it is here if anywhere that we are going to hear the voice of Paul himself and meet with his personal convictions – convictions that are carried forward with a heightened sense of individual identity.

On the other hand, this extension of the 'sender' is formulated in a way which makes Paul a mere instrument of a higher authority (Christ) and a higher cause (the Gospel). Having stated that his office is related to the 'message of God' at the end of v. 1, Paul goes on to describe the nature and content of this message in vv. 2–6. The term Gospel recurs and its interpretation is continued in 1:9,16–17. In 2:16 Paul's personal commitment to, and understanding of, the Gospel results in the phrase 'according to my gospel'. At the end of the letter body, in 15:16,19, we find the term another time in the context of a solemn statement about Paul's sense of calling (and of personal achievement). Apart from this 'apostolic' line, the term serves to mark the problem of chapters 9–11, the fact that most Jews have not responded to but rather resisted the call of the Gospel (see 10:16 and 11:28), an observation which underlines the importance of these three chapters as an integral part of the letter and not as a digression or side-track, let alone a later addition.

We learn from all these observations that Romans is no private letter or 'letter of friendship' like many letters of Cicero or of Pliny the Younger, but rather an 'ambassadorial letter'[2] in the service of the proclamation of the Gospel and that it is centred on this Gospel and expounds it – in a way that is closely connected with Paul's understanding of himself and his office. The term *apostolos* is taken up by the abstract noun *apostolé* 'apostleship' in v. 5. We wonder why this function of Paul had to be underlined in such a way, and we may guess that memories of opposition against this claim of Paul came to his mind when he started to write this letter (probably at Corinth where his apostleship had been disputed by some; see 2 Cor.: 10–12). After all, his plans in Rome and beyond Rome could only be realized in cooperation with a church that acknowledged his authority.

---

[2] See Robert Jewett, 'Romans as an Ambassadorial Letter', *Interp.* 36 (1982), 5–20.

However, by introducing himself as a 'servant of Christ Jesus' and 'called apostle set aside for the proclamation of the message of God', Paul is not only claiming an authority, he also builds a bridge of solidarity between himself and the addressees. They, too, are 'called by Jesus Christ' (v. 6) and 'called to be holy', i.e., dedicated to God (v. 7). They already share the grace that is connected with the name of the Lord Jesus Christ and the peace from God our (common) Father, blessings which Paul is only strengthening by these words. Any reader who came across a copy of this letter and read this opening could immediately understand that it came from a religious movement, and any *informed* reader could recognise it as a piece of correspondence between *Christians* (a term which Paul never uses in his letters). Jesus Christ is mentioned no less than four times in these verses (1, 4, 6, 7), twice hailed as 'our Lord' – the one who unites Paul and his readers as followers of the same master (5 and 7). Note: the lengthy expansion of the 'sender' unit of this opening does betray a rather strong 'I', but this 'I' stands in the shadow of a much bigger 'He'. The most conspicuous concern of this letter is to explain the importance of Jesus.

This importance has antecedents which Paul indicates in v. 2 before summarising its content: the Gospel which Paul has to proclaim had been *announced by prophets* whose predictions had been preserved *in holy writings*. No doubt Paul is referring to the holy Scriptures of Israel. Although a 'gospel' is by definition about a decisive (and happy) new event, it need not come unexpected. The opposite is true for people who know their Old Testament: the prophet Isaiah had predicted a time when messengers would bring 'good tidings to Zion' (Isa. 40:9; 52:7; cf. Nahum 2:1 [1:15]). Paul explicitly quotes this tradition in Rom. 10:15 and identifies the 'word of Christ' (10:17) which he preaches with these 'good tidings' announced by the prophet. It is rather astonishing that Paul anticipates this line of thought at such an early stage, in the very first sentence of the letter. As a matter of fact, it hints at a very significant feature of Romans: the theology of this letter is to a large degree *Biblical theology*, i.e., a dialogue between the Old and the New Testaments. Again and again Paul attempts to trace a continuity between the canonical literature of Judaism and the new teachings of the Jesus movement of which he is such an active part. These attempts are not restricted to quotations from Scripture which happen to fit well into a New Testament narrative (as in many instances in Matthew). They include lengthy and sophisticated arguments which – by ingenious combinations between different passages from the Bible – try to solve real problems which arise from tensions between the old faith of Israel (and its early Jewish interpretations) on one hand, and early Christian convictions on the other. Large parts of Romans, especially in chapters 3–4 and 9–11, are dedicated to these efforts of Paul. Whether he had been trained to become a 'sage' or not, he is working really hard at this task, and to understand these passages in Romans we, too, have to strain our brains in order to grasp his points and to evaluate the plausibility of his argument in the eyes of his ancient contemporaries.

But v. 2 introduces us not only to (a characteristic aspect of) Paul's way of doing theology, i.e., his exegetical approach to theological problems. It also places a signature before the whole story of the Gospel that he is going to expound. It points to the fact that the Gospel forms part of a history which God has had with his people of Israel and which he is continuing in the story of Christ and which the Gospel will not contradict or leave behind. That is the great theme of Rom. 9–11, but not only of these chapters. As early as in 3:1 we find a first attempt to redefine the special role of Israel – interrupting a context which aims primarily to show the equality of all human beings, whether Jew or Gentile, in God's sight. The evidence which Paul adduces to ground his interpretation of the Gospel in the Old Testament does not pick out strange sayings from the periphery but centres on the person of Abraham, the first of the fathers who experienced God's election (see chapter 4). And near the end, in 15:1–13, Paul binds the threads of inner-Christian exhortations together with his teaching about Israel. So that turns out to be a real concern of the whole letter. While the letter to the Galatians shares parts of the exegetical argument of Romans, it sometimes sounds more like a document of 'the parting of the ways' between Christians and Jews. The theology of Romans reveals a shift of emphasis towards staying together and continuing the dialogue.

The christology of Romans makes no exception to this rule. When Paul introduces Christ as *the* topic of his message in vv. 3–4, he uses the term 'son of God' both as a heading (in v. 3) and as a climax of what he says (in v. 4). Not a few exegetes of the twentieth century (including Jewish scholars) were convinced that by applying this title to Jesus of Nazareth, Paul crosses the border between Judaism and pagan mythology, thus moving the centre of gravity of Christian thinking away from its Biblical roots.[3] But the way in which Paul introduces this term here forbids such a verdict: Paul makes haste to base the meaning of Christ's being the son of God on an ancient and hallowed Jewish tradition – the expectation of a 'son of David', a descendant of the founder of the dynasty of Jerusalem to whom and through whom God was to restore Israel's independence under his blessing. Is that only a concession to Jewish Christians at Rome (some of whom are mentioned in the greetings of chapter 16) whose support the apostle wants to secure (or whom he simply could not ignore because of their strong influence in Rome: chapter 14)? Of course, Paul was capable of such diplomatic considerations. But he strikes this chord not only in 1:3, where compliments would be conventional, but also in one of the last verses of the letter body (15:12), thus underlining its importance – as a *distinctive* concern of Romans! For, apart from the stories about the birth of Christ, there are not too many references to his Davidic descent in the New Testament, and the only parallel (a very near one) within the Pauline letters (2 Tim. 2:8) is usually explained as an echo of Rom. 1:3 in a writing of one of Paul's co-workers or pupils.

Christ's Davidic descent is in no wise downgraded by the following statement of v. 4 that only the resurrection installed Jesus as 'son of God in power'. From the first generation of 'sons of David' descent alone could not guarantee a person's claim to the throne: only one could be elected and had to be proclaimed, beginning with Solomon. It is along this line that the resurrection marks the basis and the beginning of Christ's being 'son of God in power'. In fact, the idea of v. 4 can be explained as the result of a special reading of Nathan's prophecy in 2 Sam. 7:12–14, where David receives the promise that God will raise up his offspring and cherish him as His

[3] See H. J. Schoeps, *Paul. The Theology of the Apostle in the Light of Jewish Religious History* (London, 1961).

son. This 'raise up' originally meant 'to bring into existence'; but obviously Paul and other early Christians understood it to mean 'raise from the dead'.

Thus the Davidic christology of Rom. 1:3–4 turns out to be a crucial example of the continuity between the Holy Scriptures of old and the Gospel of Christ which Paul proclaims (see v. 2). The same conjunction recurs in Rom. 15, where Paul rounds off his letter by stressing the abiding relevance of Scripture (v. 4) and by defining the mission of Jesus to Israel as the confirmation and fulfilment of the promises given to Israel's ancestors (v. 8). The quotation of a 'Davidic' verse from Isa. 11:10 in Rom. 15:12 fits well into this picture. The christology of Romans that is given prominence by this *inclusio* (i.e., framing or returning to the beginning) is thoroughly *messianic* and thus – compared with later developments of christology – clearly Jewish–Christian.

However, that does not mean that it is narrow or conservative, limiting the mission of Christ to the Jewish nation and to a political redemption and a restoration of past glory. As the continuation in v. 5 demonstrates, the very call of Paul binds these two ends together: messianism and universalism. The exalted son of David had entrusted him with the task of preaching the Gospel to non-Jews (see Gal. 1:16), whether or not he had grasped this meaning of his calling from the beginning (see Acts 22:17–21). Within Romans he reiterates this commission in 11:13 and in a closing statement in 15:14–21 (together with 1:5 another *inclusio* holding the letter together).

In the situation given when Paul wrote his letter, the acceptance of Gentile Christians as full members of the Church was still at stake. Therefore Paul had to devote large parts of his argument to the vindication of this universalism of the Gospel (see especially Rom. 1:16 – 5:21, but also Rom. 9:6–33 and 15:9–11).

When reading Romans, it is of decisive importance to keep that in mind: what we take for granted after centuries of a mainly Gentile Christianity was the *weak position* of Paul's day, and it is due to the success of this letter that the weak position became the strong one in the course of Church history. The theology of Romans is a dynamic process trying to lead reluctant fellow-believers to new insights into the scope and the depth of God's great enterprise connected with the name of Jesus Christ. The force of Paul's argument will not be appreciated sufficiently unless we understand this 'rhetorical situation' and distinguish between the points given and the envisaged results – and the stratagems he uses.

The opening of Romans itself reflects such a movement: vv. 3–4 summarise the basic convictions which the resurrection of Jesus created in his disciples – his election as Messiah from the house of David and his exaltation as Lord (see 10:9). The truth of v. 5 – that the risen Lord calls for recognition by people from all nations and that he sends messengers (such as Paul) into the pagan world – was not evident from the beginning, and the Church of Jerusalem needed some time (and divine intervention) in order to learn it (see Acts 10–15). Even Gentiles who originally had grasped this truth and hailed this invitation to join the Church could fall back behind it when some Jewish-Christian missionaries confronted them with their claim that only members of the people of Israel (by birth or by conversion to its Law) could be sure of salvation. Paul's Letter to the Galatians and Philippians 3 are passionate counter-attacks of the apostle against this narrowing of the Gospel (disguised as its 'complementation'; see Gal. 3:3). In Romans Paul is still fighting at this front, but in a more prudent and humane way. (The fierceness of his polemics in Galatians and Phil. 3 is sometimes frightening – at least to us: for Martin Luther it was very much to his taste!) Now Paul makes more efforts to convince the reluctant and to disperse doubts. But the aim is the same: to make plain to all that faith in Christ alone is what matters when people want to be right with God. So this is a sufficient description of his commission according to v. 5: the 'obedience of faith among all nations (or Gentiles) regarding his name'. It was not necessary to give the opposite view a platform at this place; obedience to the Law (of Moses in order to attain full membership in the one and only people of God) would be discussed at length in chapters 2–4 and 7. On the other hand, it is Paul's insistence on faith in Christ that heightens the problem of Israel's unbelief and necessitates the argument of chapters 9–11 (which includes another passage on the nature and importance of faith in chapter 10).

The universalism implied in the role of faith as the one and only way to salvation is explicitly highlighted in Rom. 1:16–17, a text that is generally accepted as the 'motto' or 'thesis' or 'major proposition' of the whole letter.

The combination of 'obedience' and 'faith' in 1:5 is sometimes interpreted as an anticipation of the two unequal halves of Romans: the 'doctrinal part' of chapters 1–11 and the 'ethical part' of chapters 12–15. Although this seems to make good sense, it is probably not what Paul wants to say here. In the context of these verses it is more plausible to read it in the line of 'faith as the adequate and required response to the Lordship of Jesus'.

For those who are looking for something like the (all too) often quoted formula *indicative and imperative* in this opening of Romans, I recommend the conjunction of 'loved by God' and 'called to be holy' in v. 7. In fact, the love of God is the basis and core of the Gospel (see 5:8; 8:31–39) and 'holiness' or 'sanctification' is one of the leading notions of Paul's ethical instruction (see 6:19,22; 12:1).

The greeting in the second half of v. 7 is the typical Pauline formula proclaiming peace from God bracketed by the proclamation of grace from our Lord Jesus Christ. That the form is chiastic – linking grace to Christ and peace to God – is confirmed by texts linking peace with God (e.g., Rom. 15:33; 16:20) and by a comparison with the concluding benedictions of all undisputed letters of Paul: 'The grace of the (or our) Lord Jesus Christ[4] be with you (or with your spirit).'[5] While a wish of peace was conventional in the Ancient Near East, including Israel (and still is today), the addition of 'grace' is due to the special message which Paul is going to unfold in the course of the letter. The idea of grace is certainly not his invention, but part of the older Biblical tradition shared by Early Judaism and Early Christianity. But the *term* 'grace' occurs much more frequently in the Pauline literature (including disputed letters) than anywhere else. Romans alone contains 25 of 156 instances in the New Testament! This special liking for 'grace' is rooted in Paul's dramatic biography: having been a relentless persecutor of disciples of Jesus in his early years, he had encountered the Risen Lord not as a revengeful judge. Instead of the punishment he deserved,

---

4 'Christ' is missing only in Rom. 16:20 and 1 Cor. 16:23.

5 2 Cor. 13:13 adds 'and the love of God and the communion of the Holy Spirit' and (you) 'all'. See Jeffrey A. D. Weima, *Neglected Endings. The Significance of the Pauline Letter Closings* (1994), 80: table 1.

he was entrusted with a new and better commission. That is what Paul is alluding to in v. 5 with the phrase 'we received grace and apostleship' (see Gal. 1:15: God 'called me by his grace'; 1 Cor. 15:9–10: 'I do not deserve to be called an apostle, because I persecuted the church of God. But by the grace of God I am what I am . . .'; Rom. 15:15: 'because of the grace God gave me to be a minister of Christ Jesus to the Gentiles . . .'). Within the argument of Romans, the appeal to grace as the principle of salvation (see 3:24; 4:4, 16; 5:2,15, 17, 20, 21) is Paul's answer to those who tried to introduce the fulfilment of certain requirements of the Law of Moses (the 'works of the law', see Rom. 3:20, 28) as a condition of salvation (see Acts 15:1, 5). It is this antithesis which binds Romans closely together with Galatians (see e. g., Gal. 5:3–5).

The conjunction of faith and grace in Galatians and Romans – as opposed to (distinctively Jewish) actions required by the Law – inspired Martin Luther in his struggle against the eclipse of the Gospel in the late Middle Ages. Hence the catchwords '*sola fide, sola gratia*' as hallmarks of the Protestant Reformation. Luther's rediscovery of Paul's interpretation of the Gospel (applied to spiritual problems different from those of Paul's day) resounds in the popular hymn 'Amazing grace'. If only the message of this song could reach the minds and hearts of those who so much like to listen to it!

CHAPTER 3

Theology in process: an outline of the argument of the letter-body

A writing of the length and richness of Paul's letter to the Romans demands some help for the readers. The traditional division by chapters and verses is not from the pen of the apostle (not even the punctuation is!) and is not the only one in history: there are manuscripts of Romans with twenty instead of sixteen chapters.[1] Likewise the headlines which we find in many Bibles are not original but of later origin and vary considerably. As a rule, they give us catchwords which help us to find passages which we remember – not clear definitions of the problems discussed or summaries of the conclusions. So how can we detect structures and developments within the steady flow of sentence after sentence? Fortunately, a number of formal criteria and functional markers help us to distinguish levels of language, lines of thought, and changes of topic. That is why there is almost general agreement about the major parts of the letter, beginning with the distinction between a more doctrinal part in chapters 1–11 (climaxed by a theocentric doxology in 11:33–36) and a body of exhortations in chapters 12:1–15:13.

Doubts and discussions about the exact limits of some subdivisions result from the fact that time and again Paul introduces the problem or topic of a following passage in the last lines of the preceding one (cf. Rom. 3:20 with 3:21–30, Rom. 4:25 with chapter 5 or Rom. 5:20 with chapter 6). This procedure creates a remarkable coherence of the letter and leaves little room for complicated theories of a later compilation of the letter by a redactor. But it does not conceal the concluding character of certain sentences and the

---

[1] See Nestle-Aland, *Novum Testamentum Graece* (Stuttgart: Deutsche Bibelgesellschaft, 1993), 27th edn, 78*–79* and inner margins.

beginnings of new lines of argument. In the case of the transition from chapter 5 to chapter 6 the eschatological perspective ('eternal life') and the fully fledged christological title 'Jesus Christ our Lord' are such markers of the end of a passage, while the interrupting question 'What shall we say, then?' and the rhetorical question 'Shall we go on sinning . . .?' announce a new round of the discussion. Similarly, chapter 6 ends with the words 'eternal life in Christ Jesus our Lord' and chapter 7 begins with a rhetorical question. In the closing words of chapter 8 the eschatological perspective is less explicit, but the christological formula 'Christ Jesus our Lord' marks the end of a passage, while the opening of chapter 9 clearly announces a new topic.

In other places the traditional division of the letter into chapters is less compelling: Rom. 3:31 can be regarded as a closing statement of the preceding passage (see 3:21) or as an introduction to the appeal to Scripture in chapter 4. In the case of chapters 14–15 there is no convincing reason to see a caesura between 14:23 and 15:1. It would have been better to end with 15:6 ('. . . so that . . . you may glorify the God and Father of our Lord Jesus Christ') and to start a new chapter with the admonition of 15:7 – or to extend the chapter to the obvious end of the letter body in 15:13.

The use of questions which mark a halt within the ongoing discussion of a topic helps to identify smaller units of the argument; see 3:1, 9; 4:1; 6:15; 7:7, 13; 8:31; 9:14, 30; 11:1, 11. These questions often introduce the rebuttal of possible objections or take precautions against misunderstandings of what has been said before. The answers as a rule contribute to a further elaboration or deepening of Paul's thought or prepare the way to a discussion of new topics.

As for the style of Paul's argument, Rudolf Bultmann introduced a useful comparison with a style of philosophical discourse called *diatribe*.[2] In recent years categories of ancient rhetoric have become more popular as guidelines for our understanding the structure of Paul's letters.[3] They are useful inasmuch as they offer accepted

---

[2] See R. Bultmann, *Der Stil der paulinischen Predigt und die kynisch-stoische Diatribe* (Göttingen: Vandenhoeck and Ruprecht, 1910); S. K. Stowers, *The Diatribe and Paul's Letter to the Romans* (Chico: Scholars, Press 1981).

[3] As for their application to Romans, see W. Wuellner, 'Paul's Rhetoric of Argument in Romans: An Alternative to the Donfried-Karris Debate over Romans', in *The Romans*

terms for specific observations in the texts. They can lead astray when preconceived ideas are maintained against the evidence instead of correcting or refining a hypothesis that does not prove helpful. Above all, we must keep in mind that general rules can obscure the distinctive features of an individual phenomenon. If we are right in reckoning that Paul had a bundle of purposes in mind when writing to the Romans, then we must also expect a unique mixture of rhetorical devices. After all, his whole function as an apostle of Christ was a novelty to the ancient world, which is likely to have transformed traditional modes of speech and methods of communication.[4]

Now let us try to delineate the development of Paul's argument in the body of the letter. But where does it begin? After the initial greeting, reflections on the relation between sender and addressees of a letter such as in Rom. 1:8–15 are conventional parts of the letter framework. But in the case of Romans certain distinctive topics of this letter are silently introduced already within the opening formulas and afterwards reaffirmed by repetition in the course of the introduction. We observe a special emphasis concerning the topics *euangelion* (gospel) in vv. 9, 15, 16 and *believing* (or *faith*) in vv. 5, 8, 12, 16, 17), both centred on Jesus Christ, the son of God (see vv. 3, 4, 9) and relevant for people from all nations (see vv. 5, 14, 16, 17). These lines converge more or less in vv. 16–17, and reappear in various places of the letter-body. That is why vv. 16–17 (or sometimes only 16 or 16–18) are regarded as the 'theme' or 'motto' or 'proposition' of Romans. They should not be misunderstood as a 'definition' of the Gospel in a philosophical sense; instead they announce the personal emphasis of Paul's presentation and practice of the Gospel which he hopes to continue during his envisaged visit to the city: the Gospel is not a mere doctrine, giving some information about God and human life, but a dynamic 'speech act' of God in his creative communication with human beings, calling for a trustful response and promising to make human beings whole and secure

---

Debate. Revised and Expanded Edition, ed. Karl P. Donfried (Peabody, Mass.: Hendrickson, 1991), 128–146; R. Jewett, 'Following the Argument of Romans', ibid., 265–277; D. E. Aune, 'Romans as a Logos Protreptikos', ibid., 278–296.

[4] Paul's own critical comments on rhetorical art (such as 1 Cor. 2:1–4) must not be overestimated because disclaimers of this kind were a commonplace of ancient rhetoric!

from destructive powers which are threatening them. And, to note
a distinctive idea of Romans, this healing or saving performance of
the Gospel is the outcome of God's being 'right' in his actions (not
only 'just' or 'righteous'), and it shows people the 'right' way that
leads to life instead of death – the way of faith.

But why is a healing or rescuing act of God necessary? The rest
of the first chapter (vv. 18–32) develops a picture of mankind at odds
with God, neglecting their creator and therefore also neglected by
him, losing contact with the source of life and beauty, sinking deeper
and deeper into disorder and disgrace. The pieces of this puzzle are
taken from traditional Jewish polemics against the Gentiles who do
not know the true and living God. Therefore it can be assumed that
in this passage Paul is starting his argument on common ground
with his readers and even with his Jewish-Christian critics.

A sudden shift occurs when the second chapter addresses someone who shares Paul's verdict on mankind – but also the vices which
Paul had condemned. The judgement of God (topic of the headline in 1:18 and opposed to his saving 'rightness' of 1:17) is solemnly
declared over all who disregard the will of God – be they Gentiles
or Jews – even primarily over such Jews, because God is absolutely
righteous and 'does not show favouritism' (2:5–11). Membership
in the right community cannot secure God's favour – not even at-
tendance of the right services (where God's Law is being read and
taught); the ethical quality of one's actual life is the only test of one's
being 'right' in God's sight or not (2:12–13).

This principle is exemplified by two contrasting extreme cases:
the positive case is that of Gentiles, who know nothing of God's
will as revealed by the Torah of Moses and who – time and again –
may spontaneously behave as God wants us to behave because
their conscience knows something of good and evil (2:14–16). The
negative case which Paul depicts in darkest colours is that of a Jew,
probably a professional teacher of the Law, who prides himself of his
knowledge of God's will but blatantly disregards it, bringing shame
upon the name of God (2:17–24). These are critical, not typical,
cases, introduced by 'when' or 'if'! The ordinary way of life among
Gentiles has already been described in 1:24–32, and the essence
of Judaism is defined in 2:25–29 as keeping the Law with all one's
heart. In reality, however, there seem to be Jews who rely on their

belonging to the chosen people of God, visualised in their being circumcised (if of male sex). It is against this false feeling of security that Paul's argument in this chapter has been directed.

The beginning of chapter 3 briefly touches on the suspicion that Paul is denying the whole idea of a special status of the people of Israel. The apostle disclaims this inference and seems to start an enumeration of Israel's characteristics as compared with the rest of the world, but he cuts it short after number one (only to leave the rest until chapter 9:4–5). What he needs at this point of the argument is a reminder of the special task of the Jews as trustees of the words of God – and a reflection on the failure of at least some Jews to comply with this task. In another anticipation of a later passage, Paul hastens to assure that God's faithfulness or reliability is not diminished by the failures of his servants. Even God's judgements are witness to his integrity and consistency if contrasted with our lack of sincerity and fidelity. This reflection becomes the springboard for another aside: a brief but fierce attack on some people who accuse Paul of teaching that there is some good in doing evil because it enhances God's glory (v. 8): a reflection which Goethe put into the devil's mouth. (To be honest there was some truth – however distorted – in the slander, which Paul resents so violently; see Rom. 5:20!)

The whole section Rom. 3:1–8 sounds like an intermezzo with several topics of secondary importance which came to Paul's mind but which do not form indispensable links in the chain of his argument. They may have been prompted by rumours such as are rebutted in v. 8 or quoted in Acts 21:21.

With the question and answer of v. 9 (both a matter of dispute among commentators), Paul returns to the main concern of his argument in these chapters: the liability of both Jews and Gentiles before God and their common proneness to the influence of sin. (This is the first instance of Paul's characteristic way of speaking of sin in the singular, as if it were a person or a metaphysical power; see especially Rom. 7.) The sequel (vv. 10–18) offers a number of scriptural warrants for the universality of sin, mainly from the Psalms, interconnected by the mentioning of parts of the body as instruments of sin. (This heaping up of Biblical quotations will not recur until chapters 9–11.) From these witnesses to human failure,

Paul arrives at the conclusion that the matter must be a problem of
Jews and not only of Gentiles (as might have appeared in chapter
1:18–32): after all, these complaints must somehow relate to the
primary readers of the Bible, i.e., the Jews. The passage ends with
one of the pillars of Paul's anthropology (vv. 19–20): The whole
world (= all of mankind) is under God's judgement, guilty in God's
sight. To make this plain is the foremost service of the Law (an
idea which Luther and other reformers used to distinguish sharply
between Law and Gospel as two distinct types of God's word).

At this point Paul seems to feel that he has prepared the stage for
the appearance of his positive message of 'justification' by God's
'right(eous)ness' through Jesus Christ for all who believe in him,
Gentile or Jew (3:21–30). The catchword 'justify' (*dikaióo*) is already
introduced in the last verse of the preceding passage (3:20) and
recurs in vv. 24, 26: 28, and 30, alongside the noun *dikaiosýne* in vv.
21, 22, 25, and 26. The reasons for this terminology will be discussed
in later chapters of this book.[5] It is characteristic of Paul, though
not distinctive, and connects the Letter to the Romans with that to
the churches of Galatia. The passage refers to the saving power of
Christ's death with more or less traditional terms like 'grace' and
'redemption' (v. 24) and does not go into details. Obviously this
centre of early Christian convictions is no matter of controversy.
But the consequences he draws about the relevance of the Law
and the relationship between Jews and Gentiles have to be brought
home to the readers and defended against critics, hence the shift
of style from long sentences packed with 'big words' (vv. 21–26) to
a series of short questions and answers in vv. 27–31. The message
of these verses is that God has put an end to Jewish feelings of
superiority over the Gentiles (v. 27) since God has declared faith
to be the decisive basis of being accepted by Him, of belonging to
Him, nay, of His 'belonging to' mankind.

Can this view be reconciled with the covenant traditions of the
Old Testament? That is the question posed in 3:31 and answered
in chapter 4 as a whole. Paul's answer is a lengthy exposition of the
story of Abraham, focusing on the quotation of Gen. 15:6 where
'right(eous)ness' is attributed to Abraham on the basis of his faith

---

[5] See below, chs. 4 and 6.

in God. A clever combination of this verse with Ps. 32:1–2 (fully in line with exegetical rules of his time and tradition) allows him to argue that Abraham's faith did not 'merit' God's favour, but that he had been as much of a sinner as David, so that 'justification' is not tantamount to being innocent but to receiving forgiveness (see vv. 1–8).

But for Paul to mention Abraham meant setting foot on contested ground (see James 2:20–24). His opponents in Galatia and Jerusalem would have appealed to Abraham in order to enforce their call for the circumcision of Gentile believers. Should not all who belong to him and to God's covenant with him undergo this rite or be excluded from God's blessing (see Gen. 17)? In his rejoinder, Paul underlines the fact that Gen. 15 comes before Gen. 17 and concludes that circumcision is not at the basis of Abraham's being accepted by God and being given a covenant, but is only a secondary sign and confirmation of this election (see vv. 9–12).

However, Paul is not content with having refuted a misleading use of the Abraham tradition. In the sequel he draws important lessons from it: the priority and independence of the promise over against the Law of Moses (vv. 13–17) and the nature of faith as trust in God's creative power irrespective of discouraging experience (vv. 18–25). Gradually the argument turns from a defence of Paul's position into a proclamation of the truth and glory of the Gospel.

That is the sole topic of chapter 5. In its first half (vv. 1–11) the apostle praises the consequences of the believers' 'justification' (i.e., of Christ's death and resurrection) as peace (or reconciliation) with God, leaving no room for any doubts or despair in view of the future. The second half (vv. 12–21) develops a brief theology of history under the heading 'Adam and Christ': human history appears as reigned by two contrasting movements – a disastrous movement through sin to death which began with Adam's disobedience (and has not yet come to an end); and a counter-movement of healing this harm by the grace of God which became operative in the obedient death of Jesus.

Meanwhile, repeated asides within the preceding passages have cast a shadow falling on the Law of Moses, despite its being given by God. Time and again Paul has mentioned limits (see 3:20, 27–29) or even negative aspects of the Law (see 4:15; 5:13, 20). Especially the close connection between Law and sin postulated in 5:20 calls urgently for Paul to declare himself on this matter. That is the challenge to which he responds at length in chapters six, seven, and 8:1–11 (or to 17). (Of course, this constraint did not emerge unexpectedly but will have been part of Paul's purpose to explain the Gospel he preached.)

In the first part of chapter 6 (vv. 1–11), Paul argues on the basis of his understanding of salvation. If Jesus died for our sins and was raised again for our justification (see 4.25), then we are involved in that event. He did not suffer in our place in order to leave us unchanged where we are, but in order to draw us into his existence of victory over sin and death. Faith in Jesus Christ means identification with Him and participation in his experience of God's power. Baptism is mentioned in vv. 3–4 as the token of that identification with Him and of the radical change wrought in the lives of all who belong to Him. Of course, this new direction of one's whole life has to be translated into everyday decisions (see vv. 12–14).

The second half of this chapter offers an analysis of human existence in general to the end that 'autonomy' or 'self-government' is not a real option. Everybody *does* serve something (or someone) of higher dignity: values that make life worth living or at least promise to do so. Your only choice is between different directions of dedicating your life. Unfortunately there are attractions which sooner or later turn out to be destructive or even fatal. At the root of such experiences is sin paying its servants with death, while God's gift in Christ is eternal life (v. 23). The whole chapter leaves no doubt that Christianity (to use this term, though of later origin) is no less 'ethical monotheism' than Judaism: hence the interchange of 'God' and 'righteousness' as opposed to 'sin' and 'wickedness'.

Having rejected the misunderstanding voiced in 6:1,15 (as if justification by faith were a threat to ethics), Paul's view of the role of the Law still has to be explained. That is the main topic of chapter 7. Paul begins with a rehearsal of the change of life caused by the believer's communion with Christ (vv. 1–6). He even sharpens the challenge of earlier statements by introducing the idea of a freedom from the Law and by insinuating a causal connection between law and sin (v. 6). What he means is made plain in vv. 7–14, where Paul describes (in the style of a personal confession but intended to convey an anthropological truth) how prohibitions produce exactly that behaviour which they intend to prevent. This psychological insight was proverbial already in Paul's day and has been so until now; at the same time the wording of the passage is reminiscent of the story of 'the Fall' in Gen. 3. Conclusion: there is nothing bad or faulty in the Law as such (see vv. 12 and 14); it is ourselves who are to blame for the weakness of the law (see 8:3).

The sequel (vv. 14–25) tries to demonstrate that the picture does not really change when people take a more positive stand towards God's Law. There remains a deep gulf between theory and practice, and even our 'best intentions' cannot be trusted or are frustrated by the actual course of our actions. (Of course, there have been more optimistic views of mankind's moral capacities. But there may be none that is more honest!)

In the history of interpretation, opinions have been divided on the question whether Rom. 7 is speaking of the plight of 'natural man' or also of the struggles and deficiencies of the Christian life. This discussion reverses the order of Paul's thought in this chapter: its topic is neither the 'natural man' nor 'the Christian life' but *the Law*, or more precisely *the weakness of the Law when confronted with human nature*. The negative reactions to the Law which Paul describes occur certainly more regularly in the lives of persons without any religious commitment. But there is no indication that the apostle feels himself, or believers in general, free from such failures. However, he makes haste to point to an alternative source of moral strength which only believers have experienced and must give way to: the power of the Holy Spirit.

That is the message of chapter 8:1–11 (or 1–17), where Paul returns to proclaiming the new situation created by the saving death of Christ (v. 3). The alternative to the Law as (in theory) governing principle is the gift of the Spirit (vv. 9, 11, 13–16) or 'Christ in you' (v. 10). But that change does not mean a farewell to the ethical standards of the Law. Instead of leaving them behind, the message is that Christians are *not left alone* with the Law, doomed to moral failure by their proneness to sin, but receive new motivations to live according to God's will which the Law reveals. Again, as in chapter 6, that is not a once-and-for-all experience, but a decision to be confirmed again and again in one's daily life (see vv. 5–13).

However, it must be clear on whose side you are standing (that is the meaning of the phrases in vv. 5–7 which use to be translated with the term 'mind').

Verses 12–17 function as a transition from these ethical questions (which arose out of the discussion of the Law) to a concluding reflection on the Christian life. The prevailing impression of the rest of chapter 8 is the tension between present hardships which Christians have to endure and future glory promised to them (see vv. 17–18 and 30). The basis of their hope is their status as God's children (by adoption, in a spiritual sense, see vv. 14–15), witnessed to by the Spirit they have received, not only as moral strengthening but also as the source of their courage to approach God as their Father who cares (vv. 15, 26–28). As human beings, they share the experience of 'change and decay in all around' (see vv. 19–24) and as believers they must face additional pressure (see vv. 35–36). But no fate or foe can separate them from the love of God revealed in Christ's death and carried on by his intercession for them (vv. 31–38).

Emotionally, the beginning of chapter 9 comes like a shock. The apostle seems to fall from the heights of overwhelming joy into an abyss of deep sorrow. But this transition to a new and complicated topic has its logic. If Christians are in a way 'married' with God's unending love – how about God's 'first love', Israel? This question is not only dictated by patriotic feelings or family bonds (see v. 3) but emerges from the preceding allusions to the concept of election (see 8:29–30). And it had been announced but postponed at the beginning of chapter 3. What is at stake comes to the fore in 9:6: nothing else but the reliability of God's word, which is also the basis of trusting the Gospel of God's love in Christ.

Paul's answer – or answers – to this question comprise(s) the whole of Rom. 9–11 and must be read as a coherent (though in a way dialectical) argument. The meaning of each passage depends on the state of the discussion in a given situation.[6] In a first 'round' Paul underlines God's *freedom* to assign to everyone his place in history (9:6–29). That included the choice of but one line among the descendants of Abraham as partners in God's history

---

[6] For a fuller discussion of Rom. 9–11, see below ch. 4, pp. 77–96.

of revelation. This process of election can be narrowed down or extended to others (in Paul's view, to Gentiles). God's covenant with Israel produces no legally binding claim, since God as creator remains sovereign in his decisions. That is the first and preliminary explanation of the situation described in 9:30–33 – with non-Jews responding gladly to the Gospel of God's 'right(eous)ness' in Christ, while Jews in their majority remain standing aloof and do not understand this unexpected turn of God's history.

Chapter 10 begins with a renewed personal pledge of allegiance to Israel, and even with compliments for Israel's fervour for God (vv. 1–2), but goes on to deplore that (most of) the Jews ignore or misunderstand the whole thrust of the Holy Scriptures (vv. 3–13). On the other hand, the Scriptures themselves reveal that the problem is not at all new: Already the prophets of old had experienced frustration from their audiences – that is the lesson of the quotations which Paul reads as an anticipation of the problem of these chapters (vv. 14–21).

The concluding quotation of chapter 10, with its impressive portrait of God standing with arms wide open while Israel does not respond, triggers the crucial question of the whole 'treatise on Israel' (11:1a): has God in the end changed his attitude and thrust his people away? The emphatic 'no' after this question commands the rest of the chapter and will be developed step by step. In a first and preliminary objection to this idea, Paul points to the minority of Jews who have responded to the Gospel (including himself). Thus a total rejection of Israel is not really up for discussion (see vv. 1b–6). As a precedent, Paul recalls the crisis at the time of Elijah, when only 7,000 Israelites remained faithful to their God.

This well-known story is presented with a striking new interpretation: not as an example of religious steadfastness on the side of this minority but as an outcome of God's grace which did not allow the whole people to go astray. This interpretation sets the stage for an analogous analysis of Israel's spiritual situation in Paul's day (vv. 7–10): even Israel's 'no' to the Gospel is under God's control and in accordance with God's plans (as a quotation from Isaiah suggests).

But how does that make sense to the apostle and – more importantly – to his readers? The answer is in vv. 11–15: Israel's unresponsiveness to the Gospel has been instrumental in the spread of the Gospel to the Gentile world and that is exactly what God had in mind.

Of course, that is not yet – and cannot be – the end of the story if we keep the initial definition of the problem (in 9:6) in mind. If Israel in a way is not the villain but a 'victim' of this new turn of salvation history, then there is reason to hope that God will pick up the thread of his promises and prove faithful to his covenant with this people. The 'seeds' for this solution are already hidden in the wording of vv. 12 and 15 and 16, while its full and emphatic proclamation follows in vv. 25–27. It is prepared by an allegory in vv. 17–24 which points to the ethical relevance of this hopeful perspective for Gentile Christians who may have been tempted to look down upon unbelieving Jews, or to think that the Church has replaced Israel once and for all. The conclusion arrived at the end of the whole treatise is that the tension between God's covenant with Israel and the Gospel of universal salvation in Christ alone is part of his providence, has to be respected, and will be resolved by God in the course of history's consummation (vv. 28–32). The appropriate answer to this mystery unveiled only tentatively is to praise the mercy and wisdom of God, who will bring everything to a good end (vv. 33–36). It is a hallmark of sound Biblical doctrine that it ends up with doxology.

Equally important is the ethical outcome of such doctrine, which commands centre stage in the rest of the letter-body of Romans. Rom. 12:1–2 has been labelled the 'preamble' of this series of exhortations because it reveals (a) the motivation of Christian ethics (as thanksgiving for God's mercy – a note that is echoed in the famous reformed catechism of Heidelberg); (b) its aim to please and worship God; and (c) its task of finding out ways of life which anticipate the spirit of the age to come, and of cultivating them unabashed by the 'customs, fashions, laws' of a surrounding world without future.

The following passages represent two types of ethical instruction: the rest of chapter 12 and the second half of chapter 13 consist of collected admonitions with a low degree of coherence and almost no reasoning, which is typical of the style that has been labelled '*paraenesis*' (although Paul prefers the term *paraclesis*). By contrast,

chapter 13:1–7 and chapter 14 offer shorter or longer arguments
to establish the ethical necessity of the attitudes recommended.

Chapter 12:3–8 gives an interpretation of the different functions in the community, using the traditional imagery of body and
members, and encourages everyone to stick to, and to develop,
his personal gift while respecting that of others. Vv. 9–13 address
more emotional aspects of Christian fellowship: honest affection
for one another; mutual respect; hilarity and patience; generos-
ity and hospitality. In vv. 14–21 the relations with the surrounding
society come to the fore, especially in cases when Christians are
confronted with suspicion or open enmity. The concluding plea for
non-retaliation is somewhat extended and even underpinned by a
quotation from Scripture – an indication that Paul is already ap-
proaching the delicate problem of the appropriate attitude towards
political authorities.

That is the topic of chapter 13:1–7. What strikes us in this passage
is the variety of levels on which Paul is arguing: on a theological
level he teaches that the state of political affairs is under God's
control (implying that it is up to God to introduce new world orders,
however earnestly desired). Then follows a utilitarian argument:
resistance against the state, whether private or collective, merely
courts disaster (vv. 3–4; see Matt. 26:52). After that the apostle
joins in with a commonplace of the official ideology of Roman
dominance: the tributes of subjected nations reflect their gratitude
for the benefits of Roman legislation and administration of justice.
That is why Christian respect for the authorities and compliance
with civil duties should be a matter not only of prudence but also
of conviction (vv. 5–7).

The rest of chapter 13 returns to general rules, especially to the
love command, now declared to be the essence or headline of all
other commandments of the Law (vv. 8–10). The urgency of all
these exhortations is enriched by some critical asides on Roman
society and underlined by a reminder of the nearness of the end
of history, visualised in the imagery of the transition from night to
day (vv. 11–14).

With chapter 14 the apostle enters into a discussion of local
problems of the Christians at Rome. They must have been a real
danger to the brotherly atmosphere between, or even within, the

local groups of believers – so much so that rumours of the conflict reached Paul. The source of the tensions were different opinions on Jewish food laws and other elements of the cultic traditions of the Old Testament. With the memories of the expulsion edict of Claudius hanging over the community as an abiding shadow, the apostle apprehends a menace to the future of Christian witness in the capital and to his personal plans in this context. Therefore, he takes pains to downgrade the issues at stake (see 14:17) – although he does have his opinion of them and does sympathise with one of the parties of the conflict – and calls urgently for mutual tolerance and respect. Nevertheless, everyone should stick to his own conviction as his personal criterion of right or wrong (see 14:23). (The use of the terms 'strong' and 'weak' for the 'liberal' and the 'conservative' party in this conflict may be an echo of the terminology of education in school, where the elementary classes were labelled 'weaker' and the higher ones 'stronger'.)

The fact that the reasons for this conflict were different grades of response to Jewish traditions allows Paul to mesh this discussion into his earlier teaching on Jews and Gentiles throughout this letter. That is why in chapter 15.1–13 the concluding admonitions in this context are merged with a final vision of the peace between Israel and the nations, united in worship because of the faithfulness and mercy of God revealed and sealed in the mission of Jesus.

CHAPTER 4

Major concerns

If Romans is a real letter and not a theological treatise in the literary form of an epistle, then we should not look for an overall 'theme' that is developed step by step according to logical rules. Instead, we must expect an interaction between the presuppositions (purposes, hopes, and fears) on Paul's side and those of the recipients (as far as Paul had been informed or thought he was). Our outline in the previous chapter has shown that he addresses a wide range of topics which were interconnected but which cannot be reduced to one leading idea – apart from the fact that everything in this letter is more or less related to *the Gospel*, which Paul mentions in prominent places as his concern. The coherence of the letter consists in the process of unfolding basic aspects and practical consequences of this Gospel. That is why all attempts to focus the interpretation of Romans under a single keyword will overestimate one aspect or portion of the letter and downgrade others. That is true of the title of Adolf Schlatter's commentary of 1935 (*Gottes Gerechtigkeit* – 'God's Righteousness') as well as of J. P. Heil's monograph *Romans – Paul's Letter of Hope*.[1] On the other hand, it is quite legitimate to observe recurring concerns which deserve a special treatment. The following paragraphs will discuss several such topics which are characteristic of Paul's thought as developed in this letter.

---

[1] *AnBib* 112 (Rome, 1987).

ROMANS AS A PROCLAMATION OF PEACE
WITH GOD AND ON EARTH

Peace with God

One of the most successful topics of Romans in commercial terms is the concept of 'peace with God', taken from Rom. 5:1 and made popular by the Billy Graham's bestseller of this title. The exact term occurs nowhere else in the New Testament, while the opposite idea of enmity against God is found in Rom. 5:10 and 8:7 with just one parallel in James 4:4. In Rom. 5:10-11 this peace with God is qualified as reconciliation, i.e., 'peace after enmity'. The only parallel to this interpretation of the saving effect of Christ's death is in 2 Cor. 5:18-21 (written some time earlier than Romans, but remember that Romans seems to have been dispatched from Corinth). So we get the impression that the notion of peace with God as the promise of the Gospel is a more or less distinctive idea of Romans.

The background of the notion of peace with God is a conviction that apart from the mission of Jesus the relationship between God and humanity is marked by conflict. In Rom. 1:18-32, the apostle has specified this conflict as an unjust and ungrateful neglect of God on the human side and impending judgement from God's side (see also 2:3, 5-6 and 8-9; 3:5-7). Moreover, the various deficiencies of human affairs in ethical terms are described as consequences of a collective loss of spiritual orientation, resulting in a loss of God's guidance (see 1:24-32). Therefore the proclamation of peace with God aims at the root of this universal chaos and promises not only to establish an adequate relationship between human beings and their creator but also to heal all sorts of private relationships and social systems from destructive tendencies.

These consequences of the restored peace with God on the level of human affairs are not only a tacit implication of Paul's Gospel but also a concern of his that is spelt out explicitly in various connections: above all, the division of mankind into Gentiles and Jews receives a completely new theological interpretation which calls for a revision of political attitudes in the struggles of Paul's time. As for the inevitable conflicts between Christian groups and rival communities or a hostile society, Paul is not pouring oil into the fire but recommends that they make every effort to live on friendly terms. Last, but not least, the apostle warns of perilous tensions between believers and tries to put their causes in the right perspective.

Peace between Jews and Gentiles

It is universally agreed that comparisons between Jews and non-Jews and a discussion on the relationship between them are part and parcel of the letter's argument. The primary background of this concern is Paul's calling as apostle to the Gentiles; therefore these passages are usually read as somewhat of an apology of his office and work. Since the majority of modern readers of Romans are not Jews, Paul's emphatic inclusion of non-Jews into the scope of the Gospel is greeted with gratitude. Especially his refusal of the Judaisers' claim that all Christians should sooner or later become Jews (more prominent in Galatians than in Romans) meets with approval (if it is not overlooked or minimised as establishing what ought to be taken for granted). This perception of the topic in terms of a 'larger' missionary concept against a 'narrow' one is not wrong, but it is in danger of ignoring the ethical aspects of the question. Of course it is Paul's contention that Gentiles be included into such concepts as 'God's people' (see 9:24–26) or 'sonship' (see 8:15) or 'election' (see 8:33) – notions which previously had been reserved for Israel. But the full force of Paul's argument – in the context of contemporary convictions – is not revealed until we recognise that for ordinary Jews of his time the Gentiles where not only outsiders and strangers but *enemies*. That is the connotation connected with the repeated choice of the term *Hellenes* (Greeks) instead of the more neutral *ethne* (nations) for the non-Jewish world (see 1:16; 2:9,10; 3:9; 10:12). It recalls Alexander's brutal conquest of the Near East which had put an end to rather tolerable conditions of Jewish existence under the Persian rule, and prepared the way for a war against Israel's faith by Antiochos IV. Epiphanes in the second century BCE.[2]

---

[2] In 2 Macc. 4:13, '*Hellenismos*' is identical with apostasy.

The other side of the coin was that in a widespread pagan tradition the Jews in turn were considered enemies of the human race – a verdict echoed by Paul in his polemics against the Jews (or better Judeans) in 1 Thess. 2:15.[3] The main reason for this negative image of the Jews was their seeming lack of sociability – due to numerous food laws, purity rules, and their fear of contamination by idolatry in the context of conviviality. Of course, the pagan neighbours of diaspora Jews were unable to appreciate the theological concerns behind the peculiarities of the Jewish way of life. But their feelings were not far from the mark: after all, Peter needed a revelation from heaven in order to understand that 'no man must be called "common" or "unclean" ' (Acts 10:28). Apart from the disclosure of righteousness through Jesus Christ, even Paul shared the conviction of other Jews that 'Gentile' was tantamount to 'sinner' (see Gal. 2:15). In view of this tradition he could be sure that his sombre portrait of humanity in Rom. 1:18–32 would be understood as a picture of the Gentiles and not of the Jews.

This general verdict upon the Gentile world was at the root of the eventual decision of the leading priests of Jerusalem in AD 66 to refuse any financial support from the Romans, and the discussion that preceded this decision seems to have been the background of Paul's doubts concerning his collection for the Jerusalem church (see 15:31).[4] The spirit of passionate love of God leading to such radical acts of separation from all entanglements with the pagan world had been Paul's own ideal before his conversion, and it is still acknowledged as the best of Judaism in Rom. 10:2 – except that it suffers from blindness (see below in ch. 4, pp. 84–5). While it is always risky to imagine a course of history different from the one it did take, we may be sure that if Paul had lived to see the Jewish rebellion against Rome (starting in AD 66) it would not have been a surprise to him. His detailed argument for submission to the political status quo in Rom. 13:1–7 sounds like a warning against developments which could already be anticipated in the fifties of the first century AD. It makes him a harbinger of the 'peace party' of Judea in the early stages of the rebellion.

[3] See Est. 3,13e (LXX); Josephus, *Ant.* 11:212; Quintilian, *Inst. Or.* III 7:21; Tacitus, *Hist.* V 5:1.
[4] See above p. 16.

This warning is not directly deduced from the doctrinal part of the letter, but Paul's almost complete levelling of the difference between Gentiles and Jews in Rom. 2–3 has virtually destroyed the ideological basis of that cold war mentality which was then poisoning the feelings of pious Jews. Are Gentiles not sinners? – Yes, but are Jews free from sin? No. – But Jews know the will of God from his revelation while Gentiles don't! – Yes, but what counts with God is not knowing his will in theory but putting it into practice. And that can happen to Gentiles without their knowing that it is God's will, simply because they have an idea of good and evil, rooted in their conscience and secretly surveyed by God. By contrast, a Jew who disobeys all that he has learned in synagogue or may even be teaching others is no longer regarded as a Jew. In a word, sin is not restricted to Gentiles, and therefore righteousness is not reserved for Jews but offered to all – as sinners who receive forgiveness for Christ's sake. That puts an end to all feelings of superiority based on the possession and knowledge of God's Law. Statistics about which part of humanity has been sinning more or less are left aside as without relevance because more is expected from those who have been entrusted with more. Since being accepted by God has been revealed as a matter of pure grace and not of merit, the door of trust in God instead of self-confidence has been opened to all, and there is one and the same basis of communion with God for all. In a way, the end of Romans 3 witnesses to the birth of the concept of 'One World' – rooted in the message that God is not dividing mankind into rival parties or hostile camps but uniting them under the same diagnosis (sin) and the same remedy (grace).

What an eclipse of this message must have occurred so that one day John Lennon could write the famous lines – the creed of a generation – 'Imagine there's no heaven . . . and no religion too . . . and the world will be one.' The tragedy began perhaps when (Gentile) Christianity started to think of itself as the 'new' or 'true' Israel,[5] and inherited *both* the pride of that small but chosen nation over against the rest of the world *and* the traditional contempt of the Gentiles

5 See P. Richardson, *Israel and the Apostolic Church* (Cambridge: Cambridge University Press, 1969).

for that 'barbarian' nation with its crude oriental 'superstition'. While in other places Paul himself did not fully perceive and resist the temptation to make use of the negative image of Jews,[6] it is in Rom. 11:17–24 that he seems to have a foreboding of the damage caused by this development and makes efforts to ward it off.

Peace between Christians and the surrounding world

Paul's concern to bridge the gulf between Jews and Gentiles is one thing – his conviction that involvement in the saving work of Christ makes men and women different from ordinary people cannot be denied. It is already implied in his addressing the believers in Rome as being called to be 'holy', dedicated to God, a notion which carries with it the idea of a contrast to 'common' people. This distinction is deepened by chapter 5:12–21, where the apostle develops the idea of a new humanity starting with Christ, replacing the human conditions inaugurated by Adam's tragic failure. The sequel, in chapter 6, calls for an implementation of this global change in the way of life of individuals who have been allied with Christ in their baptism. Allegiance to Him means a commitment to righteousness and demands a farewell to one's involvement in vice and wickedness.

What happens when groups of people respond to such a call? When they try to live 'better' lives than their contemporaries? When they differ from surrounding societies not only in fact but also in principle, by constructing new and distinctive value systems for their communities? Tensions with their contemporaries and hostile reactions are almost inevitable. How can they cope with them?

In Rom. 8:35–36 Paul is alluding to persecutions as a normal experience of Christians, and in Rom. 12:2 he underlines the non-conformity of lives that are lived with the intention of pleasing God. Hence, some instruction on how to handle conflicts arising out of this determination must follow. To this end Paul recalls exhortations from the Jesus tradition, beginning with the advice to bless and not to curse one's persecutors (12:14; see Matt. 5:44; Luke 6:27–28).

---

[6] See Gal. 4:21–31; 5:12; 1 Thess. 2:15–16.

While this saying was coined for extremely critical situations, v. 17a adds the more general principle of everyday interactions: 'Repay no one evil for evil' (see 1 Thess. 5:15; 1 Pet. 3:9). The sequel in vv. 17b–18 calls for deeper reflections on the possible causes of conflict and on the limits of strategies to avoid them. The moral values of secular society should not be disregarded lightly and Christians should be sensitive to their neighbours' feelings shaped by these values. Paul appears to be conscious of the danger of unnecessary confrontations and provoked martyrdom which in fact did occur time and again in Church history. The reasons for violence against Christians have not always been purely spiritual, connected with the essence of the Gospel, and the suffering caused by such violence has not always been advantageous to the Gospel or resulted in the growth of the Church. (It cannot be excluded that Paul had a critical opinion of the 'unremitting unrest' among the Jews of Rome which under Claudius led to their expulsion from the city – possibly caused by Christian dissenters in the local synagogues. According to Acts, Paul himself preferred to leave the synagogues in cases of bitter controversies, and to form separate congregations of believers.)

Romans 13:1–7 can be interpreted as an example of a 'strategy of conformity' which restricts the issues of possible conflict and martyrdom to matters which are worth paying the price. Rom. 12:17, 21 and Rom. 13:3–4 are interconnected in that they presuppose a broad consensus on what is 'good' between Christians and their fellow-citizens. The contrast assumed in Rom. 12:2 may be a question more of ethical practice than of theory. (After all, the vices that are condemned in Rom. 13:13 were not virtues in the eyes of educated Romans, however widespread these vices may have been in Roman society, especially in its upper class.)

Rom. 12:18 aims at more than tolerance when Paul calls those hearing his letter to make every effort to live at peace with everyone. Peace is more than the absence of war or violence. It means to live on good terms with others, communicating with trust and respect on the basis of honesty and justice. Its basis is a mutual understanding, and therefore Christians cannot force their fellow-citizens into this sort of relationship. But Christians should not fall short of what they themselves can contribute to it.

Peace within and between Christian congregations

After all we have already seen, it cannot surprise us that Paul concerns himself also with peace between dissenting factions and different ministries within the Church. This is the topic of the first series of admonitions right after the preamble of his ethical instructions (Rom. 12:3–13). From his experience with the Church at Corinth (see 1 Cor. 1–4; 12–14), the apostle knows that a wealth of spiritual gifts also means variety, and variety can produce competition, and from competition it is only one small step to conflict. The discussion of this problem in Rom. 12:3–8 is much shorter than its treatment in 1 Cor. and it does not contain the catchword 'spiritual' (*pneumatikos*), which marked a cause of tensions in Corinth. But it has recourse to arguments from Paul's Corinthian correspondence, especially the term 'gift' (*charisma*) in the sense of 'function' or 'faculty' (cf. Rom. 12:6 with 1 Cor. 1:7; 7:7; 12:4, 9, 31) and the comparison with members cooperating within a body (see Rom. 12:4–5 with 1 Cor. 12:12–27).

In Rom. 12:3 Paul commends a sober estimate of the scope of one's own task, according the individual 'credit' received from God (probably an allusion to the parable of the 'talents' in Matt. 25:14–30). Each member of the community is called to fulfil and to develop his or her special ministry (vv. 6–8). In vv. 9–10 the problem of feigned feelings is addressed. Real mutual love is described as affectionate and at the same time respectful. And it must include practical consequences in sharing one's means and homes with those who are in need of help (v. 13). All these reminders combine to produce the picture of a harmonious community which could serve as a model for society as a whole.

In sharp contrast to this ideal, the real relationships among Christians in Rome seem to be tainted by mutual criticism, fears, and contempt. That is the topic of a lengthy and almost tortuous discussion in chapter 14 (summed up in chapter 15: 1–7). The question is whether Christians should follow food laws and other cultic rules of the Jewish tradition, contained in, or derived from, the Old Testament. (The keyword that proves this background of the controversy is *koinos* in chapter 14:14, used with negative connotations only in the tradition of Jewish abstinence from 'ordinary' or 'common' habits of the non-Jewish world.) Paul's problem with this situation is that he sympathises or even agrees with the 'liberal' faction which calls itself the 'strong' or 'advanced' group (see 15:1 : 'we who are strong'). But in contrast to the situation behind the Letter to the Galatians, the 'conservative' party (labelled 'weak' by their opponents) does not proclaim their concerns as part of the Gospel and condition of salvation. This allows the apostle to re-act with surprising tolerance and to put the unity of the Church above his own ideas of an 'enlightened' view on food laws (clearly expressed in 14:14).

In 14:17 he confronts the disputed problems with the essence of the kingdom of God defined as 'righteousness, peace and joy in the Holy Spirit'. While it will have been traditional to combine the kingdom with the idea of righteousness (see Matt. 5:20; 6:33), the conjunction with peace and joy seems to be due to Paul's notion of the 'fruit of the Spirit' (see Gal. 5:22: 'love, joy, peace, patience, kindness, goodness, faithfulness, gentleness, self-control').

If there is a New Testament model for a certain measure of ethi-cal pluralism within the Church, it is in Rom. 14 that we must look. Its relevance may be due to several reasons: the actual situation of separate groups of Christians in a large city such as ancient Rome; the difficulties inherent in the task of distinguishing between uni-versal values and distinctively Jewish features in the ethical heritage of the Scriptures; the necessity of combining all forces for the mis-sionary outreach Paul is planning, etc. His decisive argument for mutual respect is the example of Christ's condescension and un-conditioned acceptance of all (see 15:3, 5, 7). This secret of Christ's mission[7] connects the ideal of (in modern terms) 'ecumenical' or 'interdenominational' peace within the Church with the message of peace between Jews and Gentiles (see 15:7–13).

The urgency of the apostle's concern for harmony within the Church is underlined by a final and passionate warning against di-visions caused by new teachings, interrupting the series of heartfelt greetings in chapter 16:17. In this instance, Paul uses stronger terms than in chapter 14 and climaxes his appeal by holding the devil re-sponsible for all such discord, while God is and remains the God

---

[7] See Luke 15:2.

of peace (chapter 16:20; see 15:33). Thus, the theology of Romans begins with an instruction on the basis of peace *with* God, goes on to develop strategies of peace in human interactions, and ends up with the promise of final peace *from* God in his final victory.

RIGHTEOUSNESS REDEFINED: A METAMORPHOSIS OF ETHICS

Preparing the ground in terms of semantics

There can be no doubt that the words derived from the Greek syllable *dik-* play an important part in Paul's Letter to the Romans. In English they are usually rendered by words with the elements 'right' or 'just'. The evidence is clear already on the level of word statistics, at least in the cases of the nouns *dikaiosýne* (Romans has 34 of 92 New Testament instances), *dikaíoma* (5 of 10), *dikaíosis* (2 only in Romans), and *dikaiokrisía* (1 only in Romans) and the verb *dikaióo* (15 of 39).[8] The topics involved are given a prominent place in Rom. 1:17, are discussed at some length in 3:21–4:25, and recur in several chapters of the doctrinal part (but only once later in 14:17). If there is a consistent theology of Romans, the meaning and function of this terminology contribute much to it and call for clarification.

Our attempts in that direction must take into account that this word group has had a history in European culture that has also drawn from sources other than the Biblical tradition, especially from Greek philosophy and Roman law. When in everyday conversation we speak of 'righteous' persons or 'just' decisions, we think primarily of principles in court, in legislation, in education, in commerce, etc., where people or actions are compared with each other and have to be treated equally or adequately. In this context and tradition 'righteousness' or 'justice' is conceived of as a specific idea (however defined), distinct from other moral values (such as love, mercy, kindness, etc.). This concept is not absent from Biblical texts, but in many places a broader meaning of this word group, or different and less philosophical specifications, can be detected. Certainly the 'paths of righteousness' under the guidance of the

---

[8] By contrast, the adjective *dikaios* occurs only 7 times out of 79 in the New Testament.

divine Shepherd (Ps. 23:3) do not flow from the idea of justice but
from God's goodness. This psalm contains no reflection whatso-
ever about whether the sheep deserve their shepherd's care and
protection or not. Likewise 'righteous sacrifices' (Deut. 33:19) have
nothing to do with justice, but are sacrifices in conformance with
the cultic rules and acceptable to God. If there is an underlying
principle behind the manifold usages of this vocabulary, it is simply its function in speech acts of approval. That is why the verdict
'righteous' or 'justified' can serve as a comprehensive positive judgement on persons who live as they ought to live in the eyes of the
speaker, or who are accepted or acknowledged for other reasons.
So when we learn that Noah was 'found righteous' (Gen. 7:1), we
get no information on the standards to which he conformed but
only the conclusion that he was 'okay' in God's eyes. The same
is true where God is called 'righteous': while there are instances
which are clearly related to God's judgement (e.g., Ps. 7:11; Jer.
11:20; Rom. 2:5; 3:4–5; 2 Tim. 4:8), in other cases a broader sense
can be deduced from the context (e.g., by the parallelism in Ps.
145:17: 'The Lord is righteous in all his ways and loving towards
all he has made').[9] That is why in Rom. 1:17 the 'righteousness' of
God revealed by the Gospel is little more than another term for
his 'saving power' mentioned in v. 16. To sum up, the 'justice' or
'righteousness' language of Romans calls for a careful discussion
and selection from the possible meanings of the vocabulary in each
case. Unfortunately, Paul seems to have taken delight in 'jumping'
between different meanings of this word group in a way that con-
founds our preconceived ideas of righteousness (see especially in
Rom. 3:21–26) – and not only ours today but also those of his
contemporaries (see Rom. 10:3).

The title of this paragraph calls for another semantic clarification, now on the level of our own terminology. What do we mean
by 'ethics'? In ordinary language, we tend to understand 'ethics'
as our system of moral principles, dominated by the antithesis of
'right or wrong' or 'good or evil'. Asked about specifications, we
refer to some general ideas such as honesty, faithfulness, respect

---

[9] See 1 John 1:9: 'If we confess our sins, he is faithful and *just* and will forgive us our
sins . . .'. By contrast, in Roman criminal law a confession resulted in a man's conviction
and punishment.

of property and other rights of the individual, charity, etc. All of
these connotations sound like timeless values that are universally
recognised. But that is a delusion. Historically, ethics are a social
phenomenon that is dependent upon the character and the traditions of a given society.[10] It is a name for the body of instructions
passed on from generation to generation by parents and teachers,
to some extent codified in authoritative texts, to some extent en-
forced, if necessary, by laws and punishments. The Latin source
of our term 'moral' is *mos* ('custom'), and the Greek source of
our term 'ethics' is *ethos* ('habit'), which is also regarded as the
root of *ethnos* ('people' or 'nation' understood as a cultural community). This close connection between ethics and society is highlighted by the accusation against Paul and Silas at Philippi in Acts
16:20–21: 'These men are Jews, and are throwing our city into an
uproar by advocating *customs unlawful for us Romans* to accept or
practise.'

The problem of Paul's day: ethics revealed in the context of election

It is difficult to decide whether this accusation was wrong or justified. After all, the Christian way of life as promoted by Paul's
mission does contain certain 'habits' which were alien to pagan society but typical of Jewish tradition. A good example is the 'habit'
of dedicating one day in a week to rest, worship and religious
instruction, be it Sabbath or Sunday.[11] On the other hand, Paul
fiercely opposed the proclamation of circumcision as required from
Gentile believers. Why did he make this difference and why did
others insist on circumcision as a condition of salvation (see Acts
15:1, 5)?

The reason for this controversy is that Jewish 'ethics' are rooted in
revelation, traced back to the will of God and part of the covenant
which defines the conditions of God's favour and blessing. That
is why ethics (literally 'customs') can be used instead of explicitly
mentioning the Mosaic Law (see Acts 6:13–14; 21:21; 26:3; 28:17).
This unique situation makes it difficult to regard the content of

---

[10] See 2 Sam. 13:12: 'Such a thing should not be done *in Israel*.'
[11] See Acts 20:7; 1 Cor. 16:2.

Jewish ethics as restricted to Jewish society and subject to changes in the course of time. Instead, it suggests that to be, or to become, a member of the Jewish people is in itself an ethical requirement that is vital to one's relationship with God. That is the problem at the heart of the Galatian crisis, behind the polemics of Phil. 3, and also on the agenda of Paul when writing to the Romans. He discusses it in his statements about Jews and Gentiles, and in his reflection on the role of the Law which runs through most of the chapters of the letter.[12]

The controversy was inevitable when a religious movement of Judaism started to win converts from other nations as did the Jesus movement rather shortly after its beginning. The conflicting positions of Early Christianity have their parallel in similar positions of other Jews involved in Jewish proselytism. Josephus, *Antiquities* 20:34–48, tells the story of King Izates of Adiabene in northern Mesopotamia, who was converted to Judaism by a Jewish merchant. That is, he began to worship the God of Israel and to live according to the Mosaic Law. However, he was not circumcised because this might have caused protest or even rebellion among his pagan subjects. But after some time another Jew rebuked him sharply: 'O king, you are guilty of the greatest offence against the Law and thereby against God. For you ought not merely to read the Law but also, and even more, to do what is commanded in it. How long will you continue to be uncircumcised? If you have not yet read the law concerning this matter, read it now, so that you may know what an impiety it is that you commit' (§ 44–45). We can imagine that the 'Judaists' in Galatia and their cognates in other communities argued similarly. Conversion to Christianity was conversion to the God of Israel, and implied conversion to the Holy Scriptures of Judaism, the only Bible which early Christianity had. There you could read that God had chosen but one people from among the nations and promised his blessings to them. The rest of mankind appeared as less important in God's sight and the best thing that could happen to a Gentile was the role of a guest or a distant spectator of Israel's worship. The option of becoming a Jew by choice if not by descent was offered as a solution to this problem.

[12] The term *nomos* is absent only from chs. 1, 11–12, and 14–16.

The alternative solution that God had inaugurated a new covenant that included Gentiles on an equal standing with Jews had to be discovered, and the Letter to the Romans is one of the documents witnessing this discovery.

Ethics enforced versus corporate identity

In Gal. 3:28 Paul had boldly proclaimed that all corporate identities (such as nation, gender, and civic status) have lost their relevance for those who believe in Christ, since baptism means to be 'invested' with a completely new role. The three aspects are not of equal importance to the apostle. He never repeats this thesis concerning gender. The downgrading of the difference between free citizens and slaves is echoed in 1 Cor. 12:13 and Col. 3:11. By contrast, the (spiritual or eschatological) irrelevance of the alternative 'Gentile (or 'Greek') or Jew' is underlined again and again (see Gal. 6:15; 1 Cor. 12:13; Col. 3:11). In Romans it is Paul's concern in his first longer line of argument (2:1–4:25) and recurs in 10:12. However, in Romans he makes clear from the beginning that the historical priority of Israel as the 'first address' of God's word (see 3:2) remains valid in connection with the Gospel (see 1:16: 'first for the Jew'). Nevertheless, the main thrust of the argument aims at the equality of all human beings before God. With other views taken for granted by old, venerable, and widespread traditions, this is what Paul has to establish and to defend.

He does so by concentrating on the *individual* member of the Jewish people (and of the rest of humanity) as distinct from their corporate identity, and as personally responsible before God for his or her conduct. This shift of perspective produces the insight that to be a Jew is not only a privilege but also – or even more – a challenge. The principle of 'first for the Jew' turns out to imply that God's election makes Jews not only the primary addressees or target group of his promises but also the primary object of his wrath if they fail to fulfil their calling (see Rom. 2:9–10).[13] The decisive condition for finding God's favour is the actual behaviour

---

[13] See Amos 3:2: 'You only have I chosen from all the families of the earth; therefore I will punish you for all your sins.'

of the individual, not his or her membership in the right community (i.e., Israel as the chosen people of God).

In order to ground this position in the Biblical tradition, Paul introduces the principle of impartiality which is enjoined in the Old Testament as a rule for jurisdiction,[14] but is also attributed to God's judgements (2:11).[15] As Jouette M. Bassler has shown,[16] there is no extant precedent in the Old Testament or in early Jewish writings for Paul's application of this principle to the question of how Jews and Gentiles respectively fare in the final judgement of God. The only exact parallel in the New Testament is Acts 10:34–35, the beginning of Peter's speech in the house of the non-Jewish officer Cornelius, in a writing whose author has been closely connected to Paul by later tradition and who in fact does betray knowledge of Paul's theology and pays respect to it.

The sequel (Rom. 2:12–13) introduces the Law as the basis of Jewish corporate identity. As Paul affirms in chapter 9:4 the institution of the Law is one of God's gifts which constitute the special status of Israel that has not been repealed by the coming of Christ and the revelation of the Gospel (see 3:1–2). But how does this affect the position of the individual before God? Paul's answer is: to 'possess' the Law (as a member of the nation entrusted with it) is not enough, and to listen to its being read in synagogue services is not enough. The only thing that counts is living according to it. That is the basis of being 'justified' or 'declared righteous' (2.13).

To people who know little more than rumours or have only faint memories of Paul's theology, this statement may come as a surprise, and even some scholars have doubted whether this whole passage comes from Paul's own mind or pen. It recalls texts in areas of the New Testament which are often placed at the other end of its spectrum (see Matt. 7:24–29; 23:3; James 1:22–25). But 1 Cor. 7:19 confirms Paul's insistence on obedience to God's commandments as that which is required of both Jews and non-Jews, and Rom. 8:4 speaks of the essence of the Law as being fulfilled in the Christian

[14] See Exod. 23:6–8; Lev. 19:15; Deut. 1:17; 16:19; Ps. 82:1–4; Prov. 28, 21.
[15] See Deut. 10:17; 2 Chron. 19:7; Job 34:19; Sir. 35:12–13.
[16] See J. M. Bassler, *Divine Impartiality. Paul and a Theological Axiom* (Chico: Scholars Press, 1982).

life. So we arrive at the conclusion that Paul, in fact, is enforcing ethics in order to refute a false security among Jews who are tempted to rely on their election, while restricting the expectation of divine judgement to the heathen world.

In 2:17–24 this line of argument is illustrated by an extremely negative example (which has been misunderstood as being typical of Jews in the history of transmission,[17] translation, and interpretation). This is contrasted in vv. 14–16 with a positive possibility (not general reality[18]) on the pagan side of the comparison. Mankind is capable of some natural goodness even apart from the revelation of God's will in the history of Israel, and conscience can function as the courtroom where God is *incognito* passing judgement on human behaviour (vv. 15–16).

The outcome of the argument is summed up and (for the first time in Romans) applied to the question of circumcision in vv. 25–29: the outward performance of the rite which marked Jewish men visibly as partakers of God's covenant is of no avail to those who do not consistently live according to its rulings, and to be a Jew is virtually reduced to nothing if not implemented by a truly Jewish life, i.e., a life that is to the glory of God and honoured by God.

Ethics discarded as the basis of salvation . . .

The result of this line of argument could be the proclamation of a 'true Israel' as a law-abiding minority of the Jewish people, comparable to the sect whose library has been discovered in the caves of Qumran, open to the inclusion of a tiny percentage of pagans who might be determined to become Jews and live according to the Law. Paul's aim, however, was a concept of *universal* salvation (see 1:16). This universalism is developed gradually in chapter 3, at first on a negative line, by a series of negative statements on 'all' human beings (see 3:4, 9,12, 19, 23) or positive options attributed

---

[17] See the widespread but poorly attested variant *ide* ('Behold' or 'Look') instead of the conditional *ei de* ('But if') at the beginning of v. 17.

[18] The 'when' in v. 14 is conditional, too, but implies that the case described here occurs more often than the case of vv. 17–24.

to 'no one' (see 3:10, 11, 12, 20). The bulk of this passage consists
of quotations from Scripture which deplore the lamentable state
of human ethics. The message thus established is that God alone
is righteous (3:4–5), while Jews and Gentiles alike are all 'under
sin' (3:9). Paul's summary takes the verdict of the Scriptures as
allowing no exceptions when he denies any chance of achieving
righteousness by observing the Law (v. 20).

For those who might not be convinced by Paul's exegetical proofs
for this pessimistic view, he will provide arguments from experience
in a later chapter. In Rom. 7:7–8 he reminds his audience of the
well-known paradoxical effect of prohibitions (proverbial already in
antiquity): there is a fascination with the forbidden which entices
us to do wrong and enjoy it. But even if we intend to do good
and refrain from evil, there is still the weakness of our good will
which makes us fail despite good intentions (see Rom. 7:14–25). Not
even knowledge of God and his revealed will makes any difference,
since human nature obviously suffers from a gap between theory
and practice (see vv. 22–23). Ethical instruction as offered by the
Law is no solution to this dilemma. In a word, we are in desperate
need of salvation in the strictest sense of the word: we need to be
rescued (see v. 24).

. . . . *and replaced by grace and faith*

Paul's alternative is to insist on grace as the sole basis (see Rom.
3:24) and faith as the only condition (see vv. 25, 26, 27, 28, 30, 31)
of salvation as proclaimed in the Gospel of Christ. The emphasis
on believing which had been announced in the introduction of the
letter (see 1:5, 8, 12, 16, 17) is now put into the centre of Paul's
argument. This sounds familiar to all who share the insights of the
Protestant Reformation. But remember, the issue at stake is still the
equal standing of Jews and Gentiles, with the result that Gentile
believers do not need the 'sacrament' of circumcision (see 3:29–30).
When Paul puts 'the Law' aside in this context (see 3:20, 21, 27, 28),
he does not speak of a general 'legalism' or mere 'conservatism' but
of the document of the covenant which God has granted to Israel.
Likewise his farewell to 'boasting' (see 3:27) is no allusion to a
general human proneness to pride oneself of one's moral achievements (and to shame others), but a final refusal of a specific Jewish

contempt of Gentiles for not knowing God or his Law (see 2:17, 23).[19]

Now the emphasis on faith was no invention of Paul. It had been a feature of what he had tried to destroy as a persecutor of the Jesus movement (see Gal. 1:23). But its close connection with *grace* as opposed to a proclamation of the *Law* (see Rom. 4:16) sounds a new note. While the mercy or goodness of God is an essential aspect of how Israel of old had experienced God, beginning with His compassion with a band of slaves in Egypt, the preference for the term 'grace' has its New Testament centre of gravity in the writings of Paul and his 'school'. It is his personal fingerprint in his greetings at the beginning and end of his letters, and a recurring element of allusions to his initial preaching in church-planting (see 1 Cor. 1:4; Gal. 1:6; Phil. 1:7). Obviously this accent on grace flows out of Paul's experience of a persecutor who was pardoned and even called into service instead of being condemned and punished. This is no mere guess of ours but an aspect of the 'Damascus event' which he himself has emphasised (see Rom. 1:5; 1 Cor. 15:9–10; Gal. 1:15). Nevertheless, in Rom. 3:24 and 4:4, 16, Paul seems to presuppose an early Christian consensus that salvation is by grace. It is nothing he must introduce as a new idea or defend but rather an argument for his reasoning. He takes for granted that his audience will understand that 'grace' is the same as 'forgiveness of sins' (see 3:25; 4:7–8).

But what about *faith*? Was it more than the initial response to the Gospel, a synonym of conversion? Was it not in need of complementation by actions taken on its basis – as James was teaching (see James 2:14–26)? For that position he could appeal to a time-honoured and widespread interpretation of the Abraham tradition. This Early Jewish tradition took the praise of Abraham's faith in Gen. 15:6 as a headline to a long series of stories describing Abraham's perseverance and obedience in various 'tests', culminating in his willingness to sacrifice his son (see Gen. 22).[20] Last but not least, Abraham's 'righteousness' became the basis of a covenant

---

[19] Of course, pastoral applications of this passage to promote humility and mutual respect are not forbidden. But they were not Paul's concern in the present context, though they appear elsewhere (see Rom. 12:3; Phil. 2:1–5, 8).

[20] Cf. James 2:21–23 with Hebr. 11:17–19; 1 Macc. 2:52; Jub. 17.

(see Gen. 15:7–21), and in Gen. 17 circumcision is introduced as
an indispensable obligation on all male members of that covenant.
So can there be *righteousness* without *covenant* and *covenant* without
circumcision?

In Rom. 4 the apostle replies to these objections with an interpretation of Gen. 15:6 given in several steps, using exegetical methods
of his day. What does it mean that 'Abraham believed (or trusted)
in God and it was credited to him as righteousness'? At first Paul
concedes that the verb *logizomai* ('credit' or 'count') *can* mean the
recognition of merits. But he restricts this meaning to the context
of labour and wages. In order to clarify what the word means in
a theological context, Paul adduces a quotation from Ps. 32:1–2
(in LXX 31:1–2) where the word is used to describe forgiveness of
sins. According to the rule of 'analogy' as employed by later rabbis,
Paul can deduce from this 'parallel' that Gen. 15:6 is also about
forgiveness of sins so that Abraham's 'righteousness' turns out to
be by grace and not by innocence or even merits.[21] Then he insists on the biographical place of Abraham's justification and of the
promises given to him in Gen. 15 long before the introduction of
circumcision according to Gen. 17 (see Rom. 4:9–12). And finally
he reminds his audience of the fact that the Law came so much
later than the promises that it can have no influence on the validity
of the promises (vv. 13–16).

Apart from these objections to his opponents Paul, too, does
not understand 'faith' to mean a single, once-and-for all act of
conversion or confession of faith without consequences. The sequel
in Rom. 4:17–25 makes it clear that it means a continued trust in
God in spite of facts which seem to contradict God's word and
exclude the fulfilment of his promises. There is even a heroic aspect
in faith as illustrated by Abraham's (more or less, we should like to
add) patient waiting for the promised son. Faith in God is essentially
hope – sometimes a hope on the verge of despair – because it trusts
in God's capacity to change things radically – after the model of
His creating the world out of nothing and His raising Christ from
among the dead (see vv. 17 and 25).

---

[21] According to our own logic we would not follow Paul here, since forgiveness is described
in Ps. 32 as sins *not* being counted; by contrast a positive 'counting' could refer to obedient
actions or even merits.

This whole lesson on God's 'righteousness' as graciously imparting 'righteousness' (i.e., acceptance) to all believers is repeated with new arguments in Rom. 9:30–10:13, again introduced (in 9:30–31), and summed up (in 10:12–13) as a lesson on the relationship between the Gentiles and Israel. This is a difficult passage with essential links in the chain of argument that are only alluded to.[22] The chapter forms a part of Paul's reflection on reasons for Israel's rejection of the Gospel and will be discussed below.

Looking back on Rom. 2–4, we realise a paradoxical metamorphosis of 'ethics' (in various senses): at first corporate identity, with its peculiar ethical implications (customs, rites, etc.), is relativised or even superseded by a concept of universal ethics or essential ethics (aside from contingent requirements rooted in revelation or regional traditions). The Pauline catchword for ethics in the first sense (which may be called 'ethnic' in sociological terms or 'covenantal' in theological terms) is *erga nomou* ('specific actions required by the Law') – a term which Paul uses only with negations (see Rom. 3:20, 28; 9:32; Gal. 2:16; 3:2, 5, 10; reduced to a simple *erga* in Rom. 3:27; 4:2, 6; 9:32). Pauline expressions for ethics in the universal or timeless sense vary considerably. He seems to prefer the singular *ergon* for positive behaviour (see *to ergon tou nomou* – 'the kind of activity required by the Law' in Rom. 2:15);[23] and the plural *erga* for negative conduct (see Rom. 2:6/7; 13:12; 2 Cor. 11:15; Gal. 5:19; Col. 1:21).[24] Most important are the timeless categories 'good' and 'evil', which recur in many places.

The fact which must have baffled parts of Paul's audience is that he seems to upgrade universal ethics in order to downgrade the contingent ethics of Judaism and destroy a Jewish sense of superiority – only to discard even universal ethics as a possible way of salvation, thus destroying *any* 'boasting' or claim of righteousness by human beings (see Rom. 3:4; 4:2). This course of argument is bound to provoke protests (such as voiced in Rom. 3:5–8) and misunderstandings (perhaps hinted at in 3:31, then spoken out clearly in

---

[22] Such as an allusion to Deut. 9:4 at the beginning of a quotation from Deut. 30:12 in Rom. 10:6.

[23] See Rom. 13:3; 1 Cor. 3:13–15; Gal. 6:4; Phil. 1:22; 1 Thess. 1:3; 5:13; 2 Thess. 1:11. Notable exceptions: 1 Cor. 5:2 (and Rom. 13:3 by implication).

[24] See Eph. 4:12 over against 5:11. The picture is different in the Pastoral Epistles, where 'good works' prevails.

6:1, 15). Especially after his daring statement in 5:20 that transgressions of the Law only increased the measure of God's grace, some explanations were needed in order to make sure that Christianity does not mean libertinism. That is clarified in principle in chapters 6 and 8:1–13, and exemplified later in the exhortations of chapters 12–15.

Ethics restored to its place and revived

It is clearly the insistence on grace and the exclusion of the Law from the process of soteriology which prompts the questions of Rom. 6:1, 15 (anticipated already in 3:8). What can prevent us from doing wrong if not God's commandments? What can motivate us to obey them if not the conviction that this is a matter of to be or not to be? These questions have been considered as the most vulnerable part of Paul's theology, especially in Roman Catholic objections to the 'Paulinism' of the Protestant tradition. The apostle does accept this challenge and offers a foundation of ethics that is independent from the Law. For him, the basis of Christian ethics is Christ and the believer's participation in, and identification with, Christ. That is the core of Rom. 6:1–11. Only a misunderstanding of redemption through Christ's death as not involving our own existence can lead to a weakening of ethical motivation. To Paul, redemption did not effectively take place 'on a hill far away' unless Calvary had become a decisive turning point of one's own life, a watershed between two directions of life's flow.

To bring that home to his audience, he reminds them of their *baptism* (which in those days was a date to be remembered – we do not hear of any infants' baptism in New Testament times). In doing so he could rely on connotations of the term 'baptism' which are no longer familiar to us. As a metaphorical usage of this term in texts like Mark 10:38–39; Luke 12:50; 1 Cor. 10:1–2, and 1 Pet. 3:20–21 shows, a 'baptism' was considered as a deeply moving experience, a paying of a price, something which caused a person 'never to be the same again'. And, to be sure, John the Baptist had already interpreted baptism as a rite of repentance, i.e., of one's farewell to sin. This traditional meaning of baptism is intensified by Paul by means of the idea of identification with Christ in his death or 'being crucified with Christ' (Rom. 6.6) – just as Israelites of all generations can speak of their having taken part in the Exodus and celebrate this identification with their fathers in the meal of Passover.[25] Moreover, this identification with Christ includes His resurrection as the start of a new life that is dedicated to God. Thus, to live in Christ means to live for God (see Rom. 6:8–11). Can there be a stronger motive of ethical concern?

Unfortunately, some interpreters have proposed that Paul is not only correcting a misunderstanding of his soteriological teaching in previous chapters of Romans, but is also criticising a wrong understanding of baptism among parts of his audience. But this theory does not hold water. Baptism is clearly not a *topic* of this passage but only a *means of argument*. As such, it could not function if its meaning in turn would be obscure or even a matter of dispute. There is not the slightest hint in Rom. 6:1–11 that Paul is discussing two different problems: one emerging from his previous argument; and the other posed by a misunderstanding of baptism. A frequent negative effect of this widespread exegetical proposal has been that Paul's call to a renewed life is weakened – as if Paul was trying to postpone the beginning of new life instead of stressing the ethical impact of Christ's resurrection here and now.

The second half of Rom. 6 (vv. 15–23) is located on the level of anthropology. Here the apostle develops a theory of human existence as necessarily serving some higher power or purpose. There is no chance of living a life that is self-contained. The only choice we have is between different lords, ideals, or idols. And the basic matrix of the variety of life-scripts is the choice between good and evil, righteousness and injustice. If Christians believe they have been freed from the tragic consequences of sin (as chapter 5 has shown), then there is no alternative to serving God – which is identical with serving righteousness. A freedom from sin's bondage without a commitment to God's will is no option.

[25] See A. J. M. Wedderburn, 'The Soteriology of the Mysteries and Pauline Baptismal Theology', *NT* 29 (1987), 53–72, 71. Wedderburn has shown that the alleged parallels between Rom. 6 and the language of Greek mystery cults are not convincing, while Jewish modes of thinking offer a sufficient basis for the plausibility of Paul's argument in this passage.

A by-product of this passage is an important correction of a wide-spread error in comparisons between Judaism and Christianity. Many people think that Christianity is a religion of love or mercy, in contrast to Judaism being a religion of righteousness or justice. They overlook the fact that already the Old Testament witnesses to God's love (including his mercy towards sinners) and they ignore the importance of righteousness as an ethical value in the New Testament – and not only in Matthew (see Matt. 3:15; 5:6, 10, 20; 6:33; 21:32) but also in Paul's ethical universe. While his use of *dikaiosyne* is only partly ethical (the other part being soteriological), the negative terms *adikia* and *adikos* testify to the importance of the ethical idea of righteousness (see e.g., Rom. 1:18, 29; 2:8; 3:5; 6:13; 9:14). Paul's paradoxical definition of God's (soteriological) righteousness as forgiveness (or 'justification of the ungodly') does not discard ethical righteousness as a central idea of universal ethics.

But can this ethical instruction succeed in motivating believers to a life along this line? Is it more effective than the Law, which could only proclaim moral standards but proved unable to convey the strength to keep its commandments? The answer to this question is given in Rom. 8:1–13. In chapter 7:14–25 Paul had blamed the power of sin over human nature in its weakness ('the flesh') as responsible for our moral failures. Here sin appeared like a demon that takes possession of human bodies so that they act against God's will and even against their own insight and conscience. Now, in chapter 8, the apostle introduces a power that is stronger than sin and which can replace it as the indwelling helmsman directing the ship of our lives. It is the Holy Spirit as life-giving power, revealed as such in Christ's resurrection, who is also able to perform the miracle of changing the hearts and minds of believers so that the ethical essence of the Law begins to shape their lives. This miracle does not happen once and for all but becomes operative in everyday decisions. However, Paul takes for granted that these practical decisions are only an application and confirmation of a fundamental decision that is implied in one's belonging to Christ[26] or being a child of God (see 8:12–17).

---

[26] See Rom. 14:8–9.

Incidentally, Paul did not invent this ethical relevance of the gift of the Spirit while writing to the Romans. As early as in Gal. 5:16–26 he had argued along the same line in order to correct a misunderstanding of Christian freedom as leading to libertinism (see Gal. 5:13).

The meanings of 'law' and the relevance of the Law

An important but difficult aspect of Paul's redefinition of righteousness in Romans is its relation to the *Law*. From Phil. 3:5–6 we know that the Law had been the basis of Paul's quest for righteousness before his conversion. This concern was part of his Pharisaic heritage. According to Rom. 9:33 the conjunction of Law and righteousness was characteristic of Israel's piety. The centrality of this topic in Romans is evident from word statistics. From 195 instances of *nomos* in the New Testament, no less than 74 are found in Romans. This frequency is matched only by the shorter Letter to the Galatians, with 32 instances. Obviously the term is an indicator of the similarities between the 'rhetorical situations' of the two letters. In Galatians the cause of the debate is stated more explicitly. In Romans knowledge of the issues among the recipients is assumed and the argument expanded and enriched.

It is all the more astonishing that the relation between righteousness and the Law is not defined consistently. Strangely enough, Paul can deny a connection between them and at the same time confirm a continuity between them (see Rom. 3:21). No wonder that in one famous case – Rom. 10:4 – it is a matter of dispute whether *telos nomou* is a positive or a negative statement on the Law, meaning its *end = termination* or its *end = purpose*. The Finnish scholar Heikki Räisänen rightly speaks of 'the oscillating concept of the law' in Paul's theology.[27]

The difficulties begin with Paul's inconsistent use of the term *nomos* (as a rule translated as 'law'). It can have a range of meanings, and to distinguish between them is of primary importance in order to avoid misunderstandings of the argument. Unfortunately, the apostle can switch from one to another rather quickly. Those

---

[27] See Heikki Räisänen, *Paul and the Law* (Tübingen: Mohr Siebeck, 1983), 16–41.

of us who have been brought up with Protestant traditions or who
approach the New Testament with doctrinal categories in their
mind will tend to understand 'law' as the comprehensive term for
God's will as revealed in the Bible (Old and New Testaments), notably in the Ten Commandments, binding for all human beings.
In Paul's letters, however, we must watch the context carefully in
order to make sure that we make the right choice from a variety
of meanings. First of all, we have to decide whether *nomos* means
a language phenomenon (a body of texts or series of speech acts)
and not (rather rarely) a 'ruling principle or power' (as in Rom.
3:27; 7:23; 8:2). Then, we can distinguish between laws in general (as in Rom. 4:15b; 5:13b) and *the* Law as a technical term of
Biblical language, the translation of *torah*. But even in this line
of meaning there is variety: in Rom. 3:19 *nomos* refers to a series of
quotations from the book of Psalms so that it is an equivalent
of 'Holy Scripture'. But two verses later (3:21) the expression 'the
Law and the prophets' presupposes that 'the Law' is only one portion of the Scriptures, obviously the Pentateuch. Finally, in Rom.
13:10 (as in Gal. 5:14) 'the Law' is summed up by the commandment
to love one's neighbour – reducing 'law' to comprise only one's duties in human relationships and not our obligations towards God
(such as gratitude and worship, stressed in Rom. 1:21, 25), the topic
of the first commandments of the Decalogue.

   This jungle of meanings can remind us again of the fact that Paul
is no *theologian* in the narrow sense of the word, keen on constructing a consistent system of thought out of definitions and logical
conclusions. In writing to the Romans he remains a missionary
conscious of his calling, facing challenges from opposition within
the Church and from outward threats, but determined to fulfil his
mission. In this context he must reject the claims of the 'Judaisers'
(our terminology) who reduce the Gospel to a means of Jewish
proselytism. At the same time, he must refute the suspicion that he
has broken with essentials of Israel's faith and its foundations in the
Scriptures. In a word, the tensions in Paul's so-called 'doctrine of
the Law' are due to the fact that he did not intend to found a new
religion, while clearly serving something which the world had not
yet seen – in fact a movement of 'new creations' in Christ (see 2
Cor. 5:17).

In order to make a rough draft of the essentials of Paul's attitude to *the Law* (= Torah from Sinai), we can try the following distinction in principle (without being able to draw the line exactly): the Law has been and remains God's gracious gift to his chosen people of Israel (Rom. 9:4), document of the covenant with its promises and obligations, binding for all descendants of Abraham, Isaac, and Jacob. For the rest of mankind, the Law (sometimes including other parts of the Old Testament, sometimes not) is the revelation of the true and living God that witnesses already to the Gospel of Christ as the invitation of all nations to share Israel's blessing and to join Israel in worship. As for the ethical content of the Law, it is a matter of discernment and continual learning to find out God's will (see Rom. 12:2). Simply to copy the Jewish way of life may seem a safe course, but will not do and may create perilous tensions (see Rom. 14). Nevertheless, the basic commandments of the Old Testament remain valid as guidelines of Christian conduct (see Rom. 13:8–10).[28]

SUFFERING AND HOPE

The economy of sin, suffering, and salvation

Paul's doctrine of justification has two major aspects, a negative one and a positive one, in recent discussions often described as 'plight and solution'. The negative aspect is his view of human sinfulness and its consequences; the positive one is the work of Christ with special emphasis on the saving effect of Christ's death. The former topic is developed rather broadly in Rom. 1:18 – 3:20, the latter in Rom. 3:21 – 5:21. A closer reading of chapter 3 reveals that the apostle has to adduce a series of scriptural warrants in order to prove universal sinfulness (3:10–18), while he needs only a few words to introduce the solution of the problem through Christ's death in 3:24–26. In 4:25 he can allude to it in even shorter form. It is evident

---

[28] I wonder whether the distinction between Roman law (binding only for Roman citizens and their mutual relations) and the *ius gentium* ('law of the nations' pertinent for non-citizens) may have helped Paul, or at least the readers of Romans, to distinguish between the relevance of the Mosaic law for Jews (including Jewish Christians) on the one hand, and Gentiles (including Gentile Christians) on the other.

that in this respect Paul can build on a firm consensus of early Christianity which had already been condensed in confessional formulas such as 1 Cor. 15:3–4. When he expands this point of the creed in his own words (e.g., as an act of 'reconciliation' in Rom. 5:1–11, or as a turning point in history in 5:12–21, or as the basis of Christian ethics in 6:1–11), he adds new aspects and draws new conclusions. But he never feels obliged to establish the soteriological character of Christ's death. The only thing he has to fight for (sometimes at least, as in Galatians) is that this is the fully sufficient basis of salvation which needs no supplement and which is denied and destroyed by all who construct and proclaim additional conditions of salvation (except faith as the realisation of this salvation in individual lives).

For many readers of Romans today, the situation is very different. As a rule we take it for granted that Gentile Christians (i.e., all Christians apart from the tiny minority of 'Messianic Jews') are entitled to neglect the distinctively Jewish regulations of life such as food laws and other purity laws, Sabbath observance, and other Jewish festivals, tithing, etc. But the decisive argument of Paul against an incorporation of Christianity into Judaism has lost its persuasive power because it has become a problem to many. How can a death be thought of as the source of salvation? At this point at least – if not elsewhere – our interpretation of Romans must bridge a gap between modern modes of thinking and the mind of Paul and his contemporaries. The foundations of early Christian soteriology seem to have been covered and concealed by many layers of later developments in European cultural history, and we must try to uncover these foundations in order to understand (and trust) the building which Paul and other Christians of the first generation erected on them.

As for the tragic consequences of sin, the prevailing notions are taken from criminal law: transgression, condemnation, and punishment. No doubt, they play an important role in Biblical texts. But, as with other metaphors, we must be careful not to associate them too directly with institutions, regulations, and theoretical backgrounds of modern times. For example, in Rom. 2:5–11 the outcome of God's final judgement will not only be punishment for crimes and vices, but also reward for 'persistence in doing good' (v. 7). What kind of court is that which combines the application of criminal law and the honouring of civil merits?

But there are much deeper problems. In our Western world the nexus between crime and punishment has become a matter of social agreement, different in one society from the other, subject to changes in the course of time, susceptible of error and distortion, to some degree open for negotiation and mitigation. In short, modern jurisdiction provides no model for an absolute necessity of a completely crushing condemnation. In addition, when we apply the metaphor 'judge' to God (and it *is* a mere metaphor, though a *master metaphor,* no less than 'father' or 'king'), we run into the problem that in this case the judge is also the legislator who in his sovereignty could dispense with his previous legislation to his liking if he wants to. There is nobody above him to whom he is answerable (see Rom. 9:20). Generations of theologians (notably Anselm of Canterbury) have grappled with this problem. Progress in this matter and a reconstruction of the shattered 'building' of the message that Christ died for our sins can be achieved when we dig deeper to discover the essential logic underneath the metaphors from jurisdiction.

As a matter of fact, there are other metaphors which the Bible uses for the same topic (the disastrous consequences of sin). In Gal. 6:7–8 Paul uses a metaphor from nature (sowing and reaping) for the eternal consequences of decisions during the earthly life. But the realm of life which has provided the greatest number of metaphors for the interrelation between active life and suffered fate might be the world of *economy*. In Rom. 2:5 the metaphor of the hoarding of treasures (in this case used ironically) precedes the metaphor of judgement with no difference in the message thus conveyed.[29] In Matt. 6:19 the metaphor of the treasure is a variation of the metaphor of reward which has been used in vv. 1, 2, 4, 5, 16, and 18. This is a very telling metaphor for a logical connection between actions and their future effect upon the doer.[30] It is not reserved to good deeds and their reward but can also be used (again ironically) for the fatal consequences of sin (see Rom. 6:23: 'The wages of sin is death'). We apply the same imagery in ordinary language

---

[29] Cf. Matt. 6:19–20; Luke 12:21.   [30] Cf. Prov. 11:18, 31; 2 Macc. 8:33.

when we speak of worthwhile activities which 'pay'. Matt. 20:1–16
and Rom. 4:4 illustrate the limits of this metaphor, which can
be misunderstood; but that is no reason to avoid it.[31] Another
metaphor for the balance between wrong actions and the price to
be paid for them is 'debt' (see in the Lord's prayer, Matt. 6:12). It is
not an equivalent to 'guilt' but means 'obligation to pay', i.e., to pay
for sin by some sort of suffering. While metaphors like 'punishment'
or 'reward' imply an active partner (usually God) who initiates and
secures the adequate reaction to human actions, there are other
expressions for the logic of human destinies which suggest an in-
trinsic force of evil actions to bring some doom on the doers of evil;
see Psalms of Solomon 15:11: 'The sins of the sinners will lay their
houses waste.'

The truth of this conviction, that there is a balance between
doing and suffering in human lives, may be hidden to the public
or even to the person involved. But time and again it has been
experienced when the active and the passive part of the balance
are a mirror of each other. The technical term for such examples
is 'adequate recompense'. One of its classical wordings is in Wisd.
11:16: 'A man is punished by the same things by which he has
sinned.' A famous example of this experience is Jacob, who at first
deceived his brother Esau (see Gen. 27:35) but later on is deceived
himself by his father in law, Laban (Gen. 29:25). Similarly, David's
crime with Bathsheba against her husband Uriah is interpreted as
the source of the bloody disruptions in David's own family (see 2
Sam. 12:11). In Rom. 1:21–28 Paul, too, follows this pattern when,
in describing God's response to human failure, he uses the same
vocabulary in connection with both the failure and the response.

This logic of human affairs may be concealed as in the case of
Job, and it is even questioned in the bulk of the book of Ecclesiastes.
Nevertheless it is maintained as a fundamental structure of human
existence that can be traced in individual lives. It had been the
dominant concern of Israel's wisdom literature (see Prov. 14:14) and
the educational tradition that produced it. The prophets applied its
principles to the history of Israel.[32] Apocalyptic writings defended

[31] See Matt. 5:11–12, 46; 10:42; Mark 9:41; Luke 6:35; 1 Cor. 3:14.
[32] See 1 Sam. 15:23; 1 Kings 21:19; 2 Kings 20:12–18; Isa. 8:6–8; 28:10/13; 30:16;
Jer. 5:12–13; Hos. 4:6.

this conviction when faithfulness to God demanded the price of martyrdom and extended their trust in God beyond the borders of earthly life.

While this eschatological modification of the basic conviction is a peculiar feature of Biblical theology, the underlying anthropology seems to have been universally acknowledged in former centuries. It lies at the heart of Hinduism (and constitutes the plight from which Buddhism promises to make free). There are parallels in Greek and Roman literature[33] and echoes in classical works of European culture. Let Shakespeare's *Macbeth* (I. vii) speak for them all:

> . . . If th'assassination
> Could trammel up the consequence, and catch,
> With his surcease, success; that but this blow
> Might be the be-all and the end-all here –
> But here upon this bank and shoal of time –
> We'd jump the life to come. But in these cases
> We still have judgment here, that we but teach
> Bloody instructions, which being taught return
> To plague th'inventor. This even-handed justice
> Commends th'ingredience of our poison'd chalice
> To our own lips.

The reasons why this anthropology has lost its plausibility in modern times may be manifold. Catastrophes like the famous earthquake of Lisbon (AD 1755) have caused doubts concerning a meaning in so many individual tragedies at the same time. But, apart from public crimes with public punishment of the perpetrators, stories of individual guilt and its consequences mostly remain covered by shame and silence. They will not easily produce public truth – the kind of truth that is learned in school and which constitutes the dominant world view of a society. Above all, people who know nothing of a comfort against guilt may not have the inner strength to face the truth of a logic of recompense in their lives, and then the 'inability to mourn' tends to suppress the reasons for mourning.

Now what is the use of this digression into anthropology? How can it help us to understand the death of Jesus as a saving act of

---

[33] See Hesiod, *Op.* 265–266; Plato, *Laws.* IX 12; Phaedrus, *Fab.* IV 11:18–19; Ovid *Metamorphoses* VIII 724; Seneca, Ep. *Mor.* X 81.22.

God? In a word, it is the basis of the term 'redemption' (*apolýtrosis*), by which Paul interprets Christ's death in Rom. 3:24. 'Redemption' literally means 'the buying back' or 'paying the price for release'. Here we meet the secret of salvation from sin: the Law that evil leads into suffering cannot be broken because it is innate in human existence. But it can be neutralised by a suffering that is not deserved, a suffering of the innocent on behalf of the guilty. The famous chapter Isaiah 53 witnesses to the birth of this belief, and the intercession of the righteous Job for his merciless friends illustrates it (see Job 42:7–9). The deaths of the Jewish martyrs of the second century BC were considered as sin-offerings that helped to save the people from persecution (see 2 Macc. 7:37–38). Traditions like these provide the background of the credal statement of 1 Cor. 15:3 that 'Christ died for our sins according to the scriptures', which is echoed in Rom. 4:25 and 5:8. Its premiss is that 'no man is an island' but all human life is part of a corporate history where guilt and suffering are shared – personified and visualised in Adam – but also salvation – personified in, and performed by, Jesus Christ (see Rom. 5:12–21). Metaphors and patterns of thought that have been borrowed from jurisdiction cannot convincingly convey such a message because in our legal system nobody can take our place in court or in prison. It is the destructive *energy* of sin that calls for a remedy such as the *redemption* through the innocent death of Christ, in order to reverse the curse of sin and to replace it by God's gift of eternal life (see 5:21 and 6:23).[34]

Suffering with Christ – and with the world – in the power of hope

Paul's terminology of justification has made history, but more on the level of theology than on that of personal piety. When believers speak of their individual spiritual biography, many will prefer the term *salvation* to the term *justification*. Their memories of 'the hour I first believed' will be associated with the feeling of having been

---

[34] It is a matter of long and detailed exegetical discussion whether the term *hilastérion* in Rom. 3:25 alludes to the sacrifice at the Day of Atonement according to Lev. 16 or has a broader meaning (which, of course, would be more familiar to the Gentile Christian readers of Romans). The essential meaning of the phrase is not really affected by the decision taken on this point.

'saved'. As for Paul, he *can* say that we *have been* saved – but he immediately qualifies this by adding 'though only in hope' (New English Bible) and goes on to say: 'We hope for something we do not yet see' (Rom. 8:24–25).

Similarly in Rom. 5, the joyful conclusion from our justification that 'we have peace with God' (v. 1) introduces a reflection on hope amidst sufferings that call for perseverance (vv. 2–5). Having been declared righteous (i.e., accepted by God) because Jesus died for our sins, we have the assurance that we '*shall be* saved' (vv. 9 and 10). To be sure, there is enthusiasm in this assurance. But it is coupled with realism. Paul is speaking of *rejoicing* in this hope in spite of all troubles (vv. 2, 3, 11). But hope remains hope, assurance is not security, and believers are not yet possessors of eternal glory.

This line of thought is picked up again in Rom. 8:17 and expanded in the sequel. Now the term 'glory' (*doxa*) from 5:1 is put into focus (see 8:18, 21 together with the verb *[syn]doxazein* in vv. 17 and 30). But the necessity of suffering is emphasised as a condition of that future glory and interpreted as an aspect of one's communion with Christ (v. 17). Likewise the glory (literally 'radiance') to be revealed is described as sharing the status of Jesus as brothers and sisters of God's firstborn Son (vv. 29–30).

On the other hand, weakness and suffering are a matter of being part of the created world and of solidarity with all mortal creatures (vv. 19–23). There is no room for an otherworldliness which ignores the ordinary troubles of human existence such as hunger and thirst, clothing and housing, health and emotional needs. By contrast, believers must be ready to face additional hardships when the challenge of Christian existence meets with hostile reactions from a society that is addicted to idols instead of being dedicated to the true and living God (see vv. 35–36).

God's infinite love as the invincible basis of hope

What can enable people to preserve a hopeful look into the future when present experiences and imminent dangers seem to close up against them? The answer given in Rom. 8:35 and 39 points to the 'love of Christ' or 'the love of God that is in Christ Jesus our Lord'. It repeats and confirms the message given before in Rom.

5:1–11, where hopeful assurance despite suffering is grounded in the demonstration of God's love in Christ (5:8). In both cases the overwhelming proof of God's love is his having delivered Jesus to die for our sake (see 8:32). It is the depth of this love that guarantees its unending validity and victorious power. A sacrifice like that simply cannot be in vain. It must govern the end of history and the end of our life stories if they have ever come under the sway of this love. Paul has no doubt that this is true of all believers to whom he writes this letter: right at the beginning of the letter (in 1:7) he calls them 'loved by God'. It is part of their decisive identity, and therefore it will also govern their eternal destiny. And since everything that is final cannot be a matter of chance, the apostle is convinced that the love story between God and the believers is something which God had in mind long before his call reached them through the Gospel (see 8:28–30 with 1:6–7).

The relevance of this assurance of God's love can be illustrated by a comparison with the story of the defenders of the fortress of Massada in the final act of the first Jewish rebellion against the Romans, in AD 74. The story of their mass suicide before the victorious assault of the Romans is well known from Josephus and from the oath of modern Jewish soldiers: 'Massada shall never fall again.' The speech by which the Jewish commander of Massada urged his comrades to take this step begins with the reflection that 'we ought from the very first . . . to have read God's purpose and to have recognised that the Jewish race, once beloved of Him, had been doomed to perdition' (Josephus, *Bell. Jud.* 7.327) Whether this is historical or not (there had been survivors of the massacre who reported to the Romans), the scene illustrates the despair of people whose experience speaks against the idea that God still loves them.

Belief in a love needs some practical proof, or it will collapse sooner or later. What is true of marriage (and marriage is sometimes used as a metaphor for God's covenant with his people) applies also to matters of faith. But, according to Paul, Christians are not in need of repeated demonstrations of God's love. Instead they only have to return to the once-for-all proof of this love in praise and meditation in order to renew their hope when it is weakened by personal distress or intellectual doubts.

There is yet another context in which the connection between God's love and hope deserves attention. That 'God is love' is a commonplace to many people – as a formula for a faith which they do not and cannot share. Although they may not live in unbearable circumstances themselves, the burden of world's miseries which fill the news is so heavy on them that they cannot believe that this world of ours is under the control of a loving God. In view of this challenge, it is essential to understand that the Bible does not teach that the world as such – as it is now – reflects the love of God. Nor does it reflect the power of God here and now. An attempt to collect a portrait of God by putting together the puzzle-parts from political, medical, economical, and ecological surveys might easily end up with the face of a demon. By contrast, the message of the love of God is inseparably bound up with the memory of the cross of Christ. It is here that God's love has been convincingly proved and unmistakably defined. Instead of throwing us and our world away (for an almighty God the easiest way to overcome evil), God has chosen to become vulnerable himself by entering into a world of violence and hate in order to break it up from within – from the very bottom of suffering and shame. This course makes love and hope dependent on each other, and it is in conjunction with both of them that faith is credible and consistent.

THE MYSTERY OF ISRAEL IN THE AGE OF THE GOSPEL

Chapters 9–11 of Romans have not always received the attention which matched their proportion of the letter. Martin Luther's preface to Romans is very brief on these chapters and contains more of a warning than an encouragement to read them. This is due to his reading them as a lesson on predestination. He does not even mention the name of Israel in this context. Modern exegesis has corrected this neglect of what had been a deep concern of the apostle (though not always and everywhere: Rudolf Bultmann's *Theology of the New Testament*[35] shows almost no progress beyond Luther in this respect).

[35] (London: SCM 1952).

But differing attitudes towards the problem of Israel still contribute to a great diversity of opinion among interpreters of Paul. In part, this state of the discussion may also be explained as a consequence of extreme tensions within these chapters. If you take them as separate entities (and not as steps of an argument running through this part of the letter) you will arrive at conflicting positions. And probably no interpretation will be able to establish a complete harmony between the outcome of these chapters and the rest of the letter. But the remaining problems do not justify the radical solution of some literary critics, who declared these chapters to be a later addition. After all, the development of Early Christian attitudes towards Israel did not move in the direction of Romans 11 but rather away from the message of this chapter. In a way, Romans 9–11 could not have been written by anyone except Paul.

A personal problem of Paul, the Jew

The beginnings of chapter 9 (vv. 1–3) and chapter 10 (v. 1) reveal an exceptional involvement in the topic of these chapters. The apostle begins with underlining his sincerity in what he is going to write. With his invocation of Christ and the Holy Spirit, this pledge comes close to an oath. This seems to be a tribute to widespread doubts concerning his loyalty to his Jewish people (see Acts 21:28). But that is no reason to downgrade the content of his statement. Paul's deep concern for Israel is confirmed and illustrated by stories in Acts which report that again and again Paul tried to win believers from Jewish communities – contrary to his having been commissioned with the Gentile mission and not the mission among Jews at the Jerusalem council (see Gal. 2:7–9). His confession of sorrow and anguish in Rom 9:2 must be taken at face value, especially if it is addressed mainly to Gentile believers in Rome, who, according to Rom. 11:17–24, might be tempted to nourish arrogant attitudes towards unbelieving Jews.

As proof of his unbroken solidarity with Israel, Paul claims to have offered himself as a sacrifice for his people (9:3). The wording of this phrase contains some problems so that its meaning cannot be defined with absolute certainty. Is Paul speaking of a mere wish – realisable or unrealisable? – or of a vow he took? Does 'from Christ' mean that he is (or would be) ready to be separated from Christ instead of his fellow-Jews, or is he speaking of Christ dedicating him (to be sacrificed?) for the benefit of his people? What exactly is the meaning of *anathema*: is it an equivalent of the Hebrew *herem*, meaning exclusion or even destruction; or of *qorban*, meaning dedication to God; or is it meant to evoke the Roman idea of *devotio* – the self-sacrifice of Roman leaders as an appeal to the gods to save their army from an impending defeat?[36] In any case, the emphatic 'I myself' indicates that the apostle is speaking of something extraordinary, an exceptional destiny he was ready to accept on behalf of his fellow-Jews. It may be that Paul's determination to visit Jerusalem, irrespective of the dangers of that journey (see 15:31) and in spite of prophecies that warned him (see Acts 20:22–24; 21:10–14) ,was due to his readiness to become a martyr of his passionate love for his people. In Rom. 10:1 the wording is quite clear: Paul's innermost feelings lead him to pray for the salvation of Israel – which means that the 'mystery' which he discloses in 11:26 ('All Israel will be saved') was revealed to him as an answer to such prayers.

Adolf von Harnack, the leading scholar of academic Berlin a hundred years ago, denounced Paul for having betrayed the logical outcome of his theology when he preserved, or rather re-established, a hope for Israel in Rom. 11. In von Harnack's view, this was an honourable act of religious patriotism, but due to human weakness at the cost of theological consistency. However, this verdict must be read in the context of von Harnack's sympathy with Marcion and of his (in)famous statement that 'to reject the Old Testament in the second century had been a mistake . . . to stick to it in the sixteenth century was a fate which the Reformers could not escape; but to preserve it as canonical for Protestants beyond the eighteenth century results from a religious paralysis of the Church'.[37] Moreover, von Harnack's view of science (including theology) as being completely detached from personal or political concerns was typical of his day, but has since been overcome. As

---

[36] See below in ch. 6, pp. 131–134.
[37] Quoted from A. von Harnack, *Marcion. Das Evangelium vom fremden Gott* (1921, 2nd edn 1924), 127.

it is no blemish for medical research to be motivated by compassion with suffering people, we should appreciate the connection between Paul's earnest prayers for his people and his teaching on the future of Israel in Romans 9–11. After all, solutions of afflicting problems usually do not come out of the blue but to those who have wrestled with them for a while.

A theological dilemma of Paul, the apostle

As for the question of consistency, we have to remember that as early as in Rom. 3:2 the apostle had set out to enumerate the 'extras' of Israel compared with the rest of the world. There he had stopped short after having stated that the Israelites had been 'entrusted with the words of God'. Now, in Rom. 9:4–5, he offers up to ten marks of distinction (if we count 'Israelites' at the beginning as honorific name[38] and accept the conjecture 'to whom belongs God . . .' at the end). The order of this enumeration seems to be haphazard, but one thing is clear: Paul is referring to the history of Israel as a story with God: 'adoption' alludes to texts like Exod. 4:22; Jer. 31:9, 20, and Hos. 11:1, which speak of Israel as God's son. 'Glory' is not the nation's fame but the term used in the Old Testament for the presence of God in Israel's sanctuary or in the course of special experiences with God (see e.g., Exod. 14:4; 15:7). The plural 'covenants' refers to the decisive aspect of God's repeated initiatives to create a special relationship with the nation or with their ancestors or particular families within Israel (such as the dynasty of David or certain priestly families). The 'legislation' is affirmed as an aspect of Israel's election that is in no wise diminished by the fact that according to Paul it is not to be imposed on Gentile believers. The Law remains part of Israel's precious heritage and calling. The inclusion of the term 'worship' may astonish those who interpret the atoning death of Christ as replacing and putting an end to the temple of Jerusalem and its cultic performances. But Paul himself had continued to participate in temple services – including sacrifices (see Acts 21:26; 22:17–21; 24:17). Most important

---

[38] 'Israelites' at the beginning of v. 4 is not just an apposition to 'my brothers' and 'my own race' (as in the New International Version) but part of the first of four or five relative clauses which expound the distinctive dignity of God's chosen people.

is the mention of 'the promises' because this term stands for the conviction that God is in control of history – at least in the long run – and that he is determined to lead his people into a future of peace and blessing. The last three topics are not abstract concepts but persons: the patriarchs as the roots of the chosen nation and the first recipients of God's election and promises[39] – the Messiah who was to be born as a Jew (and whose mind and mission would be formed by Jewish traditions)[40] – and God himself, who again and again had declared Himself to be Israel's God (a covenant which, according to Rom. 3:29–30, now includes all humankind but has not been withdrawn from Israel).[41]

Now what is the function of this long list? As the sequel to vv. 1–3, it should explain the reasons for Paul's sorrow when he thinks of his fellow-Jews. The logic of this sequel seems to be its contrast to the present state of Israel, which, according to Rom. 10:1, is outside of the sway of salvation.[42] This state of affairs is a contradiction to all the blessings which God has invested in this people. Therefore it is a challenge to all who trust that God is carrying His plans to completion.[43] Especially the mention of God's *promises* evokes the question of *God's faithfulness*. In a word, the most piercing question behind the whole discussion of Rom. 9–11 is not 'What becomes of Israel?' but – in the words of Rom. 9:6: 'Can it be that the word of God has failed?' Although Paul is pushing aside this idea in the very act of verbalising it, he will need the whole of these three chapters in order to explain and to substantiate this 'No'. In the end he can sum them up with the assertion that 'God's gifts and his call are irrevocable' (11:29). If it were otherwise, the call that constituted the Church[44] could not be trusted either. Thus, the topic of Romans 9–11 is the fate and future of Israel, but the issue that is at stake is the reliability of God's word, which is challenged by present experience. That is, these chapters are about the *truth* of God, which has to be vindicated by his truthfulness in making good the promises once made to the patriarchs (see 15:8).

---

[39] See Rom. 11:28; 15:8. [40] See Rom. 1:3; 15:12; John 4:22–26.

[41] I adopt the conjecture to read '*hon ho . . . theos*' instead of '*ho on . . . theos*'. A formal parallel to Rom. 9:4–5, i.e., an enumeration of 'properties' of the Church with God as the last clause, is found in Eph. 2:12.

[42] Cf. Rom. 11:26. [43] Cf. Phil. 1:6. [44] See Rom. 1:6–7 and 8:30.

God's freedom affirmed

That Paul's thinking is not dictated by his patriotic feelings can be seen from the outset of his argument in Rom. 9:6–29. Right at the beginning, in v. 6, he bluntly states that descent from Israel (= Jacob) is not a sufficient definition of the people of Israel (or the only condition of sharing the special dignity of 'Israelites', as used in v. 4). If the word of God cannot fail, his people can fail and did fail in the past (see Isa. 40:6–8). Descent from the patriarchs does not allow any feeling of security. Paul can ground his argument in examples from the history of the patriarchs (see vv. 7–13): the line of election did not include all physical descendants of Abraham but only those of his son Isaac (and not of his firstborn, Ishmael – the alleged ancestor of the Arabs), and again not all descendants of Isaac but only those of Jacob (and not of Esau – the alleged ancestor of the Edomites /Idumaeans). While these Biblical examples could not be disputed, his application of this principle to the descendants of Jacob, too, may have shocked some of his Jewish contemporaries. Some modern commentators (such as Ernst Käsemann) held that Paul is here breaking with fundamental convictions of ancient Judaism. No doubt, his word must have been a challenge to some Jews. But essentially the apostle is only repeating an aspect of the message of John the Baptist (see Matt. 3:9; Luke 3:8). Likewise the Essenes taught that only those Jews who joined their community constituted the true Israel. So this position was an option within early Judaism – though certainly not the only one, not a comfortable one, and probably not a popular one.

It is, however, essential for the credibility of Paul's theology. If God has chosen a family and – in due course – a people, then the danger arises that God is misunderstood as a slave of his once-and-for-all election. This would turn theology into an ideology, a mere instrument of affirming and glorifying the collective identity of this nation. And then the decline of this nation would mean the death of its God. But Paul is looking out for a hope for his fellow-Jews, who, in his opinion, are undergoing a crisis of their spiritual history. In Rom. 15:13 he will call God 'the God of hope'. Now the first article of a creed of hope in God is God's freedom, His liberty to direct history according to His wisdom and will and in complete independence from human conditions. That includes and demands His freedom also to determine the limits of his chosen people (the thesis of Rom. 9:6b). The situation of Israel, which, according to vv. 1–3, was so painful to the apostle, has to be accepted as a reality that is not out of God's control.

But that is not the only consequence which Paul draws from God's freedom. It is also the basis of an enlargement of the people of God (see 9:24–26). The inclusion of Gentiles who have responded to the call of the Gospel is also an act of God's freedom. As such, it has to be respected by those who originally opposed this development of Early Christianity (see Acts 10–11 and 15; Gal. 2:1–10). That is the final outcome of this first line of argument in Rom. 9–11. (In vv. 19–23 Paul answers to objections against this theology of God's freedom, and affirms it as a necessary implication of His being the creator of all and of our being created by Him.) Paul can in all honesty admit that this turn of God's history with Israel came quite unexpectedly. In fact, in vv. 30–33 he even underlines its paradoxical nature. All he can do in order to make peace with it for the moment is to quote words of Scripture (from Isa. 8:14 and 28:16) which are as much of a riddle as the course of events he has described. To the readers of the letter, they convey the message that even strange and disturbing developments can turn out as moves in God's strategy. Let nobody stop reading at this point before he has discovered their hidden meaning!

In former centuries, theologians used to interpret this chapter as the basis of a doctrine of predestination. That is, they took it to teach that eternal salvation was a matter of being chosen by God (including the reverse, that eternal death or punishment could be the destiny of some – or even many – according to God's will). Now Paul's insistence on God's absolute freedom and on His independence of human reactions (see Rom. 9:11–12) certainly demands an acknowledgement in all humility that God is really free to act like that. On the other hand, it has to be stressed that this doctrine is not what Paul is teaching here. The whole chapter is not about eternal salvation but about the course of God's history with Israel. The example of Pharaoh is not quoted in v. 17 in order to teach that God created him to go to hell, but only that his part in history was that of an enemy of Israel and that therefore his fate was to

be defeated, sadly enough. (Rabbinical traditions tell the tale that
God did not allow the angels in heaven to rejoice at the destruction
of Pharaoh's army – because they, too, had been God's creatures!)
We should not mix up the levels of history and eternal salvation,
although history (or earthly life) is the stage where decisions of
eternal relevance are taken. But Romans 9–11 is on the whole not
about individual Jews or Gentiles and their story with God (which
had been the topic of earlier chapters), but about the role of the
people of Israel as a corporate figure in the drama of God's history.
Paul's teaching has to be related to the questions he is discussing.
To draw conclusions from it for other topics or fields of theology is
legitimate, but demands very careful reflection.

Israel's failure deplored

In chapter 10 the specific Christian perspective of Paul comes
to the fore: Christ is the source of righteousness for all believers
(v. 4), and saving faith centres on his resurrection and lordship
(v. 9). That is why Israel has not yet experienced the blessings of
this salvation. Paul can only repeat his confession of solidarity with
his people and mention his heartfelt prayers for them. The following verses offer an explanation of the state of affairs on the level
of human attitudes and understanding. At first Paul gives credit to
the measure of religious fervour among his fellow Jews. Their 'No'
to the Gospel is not due to any neglect of God's will. On the contrary, it has religious reasons. It is the outcome of their passion for
God. Jews are standing aloof because of a marvellous enthusiasm
for God which, in their eyes, forbids them to put their trust in a
man like Jesus and a message like the Gospel. This statement of
Paul leaves no room for any moral verdict on Jewish unbelief but
explains it as a tragic conflict. While according to Rom. 1:20 there
is no excuse for mankind's turning away from God the Creator,
Jewish unbelief is in a way consistent. It is not wrong by intention
but only because of some lack of understanding (see 10:2).

At this point we have to accept that Paul knows what he is speaking of, and that in a double sense. He certainly knows his people and their state of mind at the time of his writing this letter–
although there are scholars who maintain that Paul has seriously

misunderstood Judaism. (Unfortunately they have compared Paul's analysis of Judaism with a Judaism of later centuries which emerged from the catastrophes of the ill-fated rebellions against the Romans, resulting in the loss of Jerusalem and its temple.) And he knows what he means when he is speaking of 'passion' or 'zeal' for God, because this had been the ideal behind his persecution of the disciples of Jesus (see Phil. 3:6; Gal. 1:13–14; Acts 22:3–4). Whatever fault it was which he found with the Jesus movement (and there is some uncertainty about this question), in any case he had been convinced that it was on the point of leading Israel astray and that to tolerate it could call God's wrath down on his people (see Num. 25 etc).[45] And, according to Josephus, the fifties of the first century witnessed an increase of Jewish radicalism in the homeland (possibly one of the reasons why Paul's Gentile mission was no longer appreciated by Jewish Christians in Jerusalem). While Paul had been 'ahead of his generation' (see Gal. 1:14), his former attitude had meanwhile spread and began to prevail. Therefore he can be believed to have given a clue to the rejection of the Gospel by many Jews. And if only Paul's vision of the Risen Lord (and neither Peter's sermons nor Stephen's reasoning or suffering) had corrected his former perspective of the Jesus movement, the apostle cannot morally condemn those who still share the views which he once held. After all, it is only '*now*' that the 'righteousness of God' of which the Gospel speaks has been revealed (see 1:16–17; 3:21) The only flaw in Israel's unbelief (towards the Gospel, not towards God) is that this revelation has not yet enlightened their minds.

The close relation between Paul's interpretation of the position of mainstream Judaism, and his understanding of his own biography, is also highlighted by his confrontation of 'God's righteousness' or ('righteousness from God') with 'one's own righteousness' in both contexts (see Rom. 10:3 with Phil. 3:9). In both contexts it is clear that Paul's or Israel's 'own' righteousness is derived from the Law, but not simply from their knowledge or possession of the Law but conditioned by one's actual observance of the Law (see Rom. 10:5; Phil. 3:6). Now what is the fly in the ointment of a life that is dedicated to this ideal? Next to nothing – as long as Jesus Christ

---

[45] See above pp. 6–8.

had not appeared on the scene of history (and in Paul's life)! In
Phil. 3:8 the hard verdict 'rubbish' or 'garbage' (or worse) does
not refer to Paul's former law-observant life *as such*, but only to its
inferiority as compared with Paul's later knowledge of Christ and
participation in his sufferings and resurrection. Likewise in Rom.
10:5–13 the contrast to a literal understanding of the Law as a set of
commandments and nothing else is an interpretation of Scripture
as pointing to Christ. (If this exegesis sounds fanciful to us, this
impression must not be dated back to Paul's day, when creative
interpretation was also cultivated by Jewish authors like Philo of
Alexandria.)

We must, however, keep in mind the earlier chapters of Romans,
where the apostle has demonstrated that possession of the Law does
not prevent people from sinning. In the light of this argument, Paul's
evaluation of his former life as 'faultless' in terms of righteousness
according to the Law (see Phil. 3:6) should be read as a quotation
of his former self-confidence and not as a truth he subscribes to
from his Christian point of view. That this applies not only to him
personally but to all of Israel is hinted at in a very casual way by a
quotation which most Bible-readers of today will fail to notice. In
Rom. 10:6 Paul's quotation from Scripture is introduced by: 'Do
not say in your heart'. What follows (and only that) is taken from
Deut. 30:12–13. The introduction itself is a quotation from Deut.
9:4, which should be read as if Paul was saying 'see Deut. 9' (there
were no numbers for chapter and verse in his Bible). There Israel
is warned three times (in vv. 4, 5, and 6) against thinking that the
gift of the land of Canaan is a reward for Israel's righteousness
compared with the wickedness of the Canaanites! Thus the idea
of *meriting* God's favour is excluded by the Law itself right at the
beginning of Israel's existence as a nation!

That is why Paul can write as a headline to this whole line of
scriptural argument: 'What the law is all about is (nothing else but)
Christ as the basis of righteousness for all believers.' (Rom. 10:4).
Many interpreters up to recent publications[46] hold that the Greek
term *telos* in this verse means 'end' in the sense of 'termination' or

---

[46] E.g., John Paul Heil, 'Christ the Termination of the Law (Romans 9:30–33 – 10:8)', *CBQ*
63 (2001), 484–498.

(when applied to a law) 'abrogation'. But this is not the primary and usual meaning of *telos*.[47] Originally a word for 'the decisive moment' or 'what matters most', it can mean the (intended or achieved) 'outcome' or 'result'. When applied to an action or process in time, this meaning can develop into 'end' as 'termination' because what matters most in the evaluation of actions is where they lead – and when they have reached their aim they belong to the past. But *nomos* does not designate an action or process. The closest New Testament parallel from which to conclude what *telos* means in connection with words like *nomos* is 1 Tim. 1:5, where we read: 'the *telos* of the commandment (or teaching) is love.' I know of no Bible translation nor of anybody else who proposes to translate *telos* here by 'termination'. Rather it is taken for granted that it must mean 'goal' or '(ultimate) aim', or 'object'. So this should also be the basis of our understanding of Rom. 10:4 (although there may be attractive ways of *making sense* of reading it otherwise; but in exegesis we have to explore the sense which the text yields before we integrate it into our overall theological convictions or constructions). Thus Rom. 10:4 is just a different wording for Paul's claim of Rom. 3:21 that the righteousness of God (as operative in Christ's death and the salvation of all believers), while fully revealed only by the Gospel, had been testified to already in the Old Testament. This means that Israel's 'lack of knowledge' which Paul deplores in Rom. 10:2–3 turns out to be a lack of understanding the Scriptures as witnessing to Christ and the Gospel.

This is confirmed by the quotations in the later verses of this chapter. In v. 16 the apostle interprets Isa. 53:1 ('Lord, who has believed our message?') as a prophecy referring to the Gospel (or the Gospel as already proclaimed by Isaiah?). Verse 18 seems to imply that the words of Ps. 19:4 ('Their voice has gone out into all the earth, their words to the ends of the world') are about the 'word of Christ' mentioned in v. 17. Finally, in v. 21, another quotation from Isaiah (65:2: 'All day long I have held out my hands to a disobedient and obstinate people') yields another anticipation of the failure of Israel to respond to the Gospel. The picture recalls

---

[47] See Robert Badenas, *Christ the End of the Law. Romans 10:4 in Pauline Perspective* (JSNT.SS 10) (Sheffield, 1985), 38–80.

the figure of the loving father of Luke 15 with arms wide open greeting his 'lost son' returning home. But what a contrast: there is nobody coming. There are many texts in the Bible which speak of frustrated hopes of God, mainly parables such as Isa. 5:1–7 or Luke 13:6–9 using the metaphor of 'fruit' for justified expectations which did not come true. The metaphorical language of Isa. 65:2 as quoted in Rom. 10:21 may be the strongest expression of God's suffering from human indifference.

The other two quotations (from Deut. 32:21 in v. 19, and from Isa. 65:1 in v. 20) take up the line of Rom. 9:30–32, where Israel's failure had been contrasted with the positive response of Gentiles to the Gospel. Both quotations serve as a bridge to the first part of chapter 11, where the comparison and connection between Israel and the Gentile (Christians) goes into the next round. However, the immediate starting point of chapter 11 is the challenge contained in the last verse of chapter 10.

God's faithfulness revealed

Chapter 11 begins with an erroneous conclusion from what Paul had written before, quoted in order to be refused at once: 'Did God thrust away his people?' The language of this question is not so much juridical (as is suggested by the frequent translation with 'rejected') but close to the image of 10:21: has God – after having stretched out his hands in vain – now turned to drive his people away with a clenched fist? (See Acts 7:27, 39.) Or, to put it in more traditional theological terms, has his patience been replaced by his wrath? That is the question which Paul is going to answer in this chapter, and he does so in several steps.

In a first step, he points to the fact that it is a majority but not all of Israel who reject the Gospel. He reminds his readers of the fact that he himself is an Israelite (more precisely, a Benjaminite). He might as well have chosen to mention some Jewish Christians who lived at Rome, as the greetings in Rom. 16:3, 7, 11 show. But to mention the tribe of Benjamin fits well into the story which Paul is going to tell in this chapter. According to Judges 20–21, his tribe had once been reduced to 600 men, but recovered again from this tragic blow.

Paul's disclaimer in v. 2 is a tacit quotation from 2 Sam. 12:22 (LXX), where Samuel affirms the faithfulness and forgiveness of God after the Israelites had demanded the establishment of a kingdom according to the model of neighbouring countries. Then the apostle goes on to quote from the story of Elijah in 1 Kings 19, where the prophet despairs of his whole mission and thinks that he alone has remained faithful to the Lord while the rest of the people have turned to the cult of Baal. In reply, the prophet is told that no less than 7,000 men have remained faithful, too (see 1 Kings 19:18). In quoting this oracle of God, Paul keeps closer to the original Hebrew than to its translation in the Septuagint. At the same time, he gives it a new meaning by isolating it from its context and inserting it into his own line of argument. While the original text means that the 7,000 will be spared from a judgement, Paul makes it say that it was God himself who prevented those 7,000 from apostasy. This interpretation makes the incident an example of God's being in control of Israel's history, including times of spiritual crisis.

The application of this lesson to the problems of Paul's day in vv. 5–10 reveals its logic more clearly. Here the implication of the story is made explicit: it had been God's decision to hold those 7,000 – and not the majority of Israel – back from idolatry. Likewise, God has decided to open the hearts of only a minority of Jews for the Gospel. The majority is incapable of grasping its truth – a fact which Paul's finds predicted in another patchwork of Scripture quotations.

In this context the notion of a 'hardening' (v. 7, recurring in v. 24) has to be protected against misunderstandings. When in our modern language 'hard' is used metaphorically to describe personal attitudes, the meaning is generally rather negative and that in a moral sense, such as 'harsh', 'severe', 'cruel', 'unfeeling', 'relentless' (e.g., in the term 'hardliner'). As the following quotations show, these are not the connotations which the Biblical usage of 'hard' in connection with the hearts and minds of people evokes. Rather, the complaint is about a lack of perception or understanding. That is also confirmed by parallels in the New Testament such as Mark 3:5; 6:52; 8:17–18; 2 Cor. 3:14; Eph. 4:18. Therefore it is no mistake but a case of 'dynamic' or 'functional equivalence' that the ancient Syriac and Latin translations of Rom. 11:25 render *porosis*

(handwritten margin note: porosis = blindness / hardened hearts / children)

('hardening') by terms meaning 'blindness' – a tradition followed by the King James Version and the New English Bible, both here and in Rom. 11:7.

Thus, the problem of Israel's unbelief is removed from the moral level (where it had been placed at the end of chapter 10) back to the sphere of God's policy in ruling the history of the people he has chosen (see 9:6–29). To be sure, already Paul's prayers for Israel had implied that God has the power to influence the hearts of men and women. But now he begins to develop an interpretation of Israel's unbelief as intended by God and meaningful in the context of God's plans. The very fact that things developed in accordance with God's will excludes the suspicion that a final downfall of Israel could be the outcome of the present crisis (v. 11).

In a surprising turn of perspective, Paul goes on to construct a *connection* between Israel's being downgraded or neglected for the moment[48] and the success of the Gospel among people of non-Jewish origin which Paul had experienced and to which most of the readers of Romans owed their own share of Christ's saving work (vv. 12–15). In other words, Israel has paid a price for the rise of the Gentile mission, and Paul does not even hesitate to use the term 'reconciliation of the world' for Israel's contribution to the salvation of Gentiles – a terminology which in other places is applied to the saving power of Christ's death (see Rom. 5:10–11; 2 Cor. 5:18–21).

As readers of the Acts of the Apostles, we are in a position to 'fill in' this theory with stories from the early mission of the Church. The very beginnings of a missionary preaching that was consciously (and successfully) addressed to Gentiles are ascribed to some fugitives from Jerusalem who had fled from the persecution after the martyrdom of Stephen (see Acts 11:19–21). And Paul and his team used to start their missionary work in every city (if possible) in the local synagogue, but were repeatedly forced to retreat from there and to concentrate on the conversion of Gentiles (see Acts 13:45–47; 18:6; 28:25–28).

---

[48] The term *apobole* in v. 15 does not mean 'rejection' but 'loss' (see Acts 27:22; Josephus, *Antiquities* 4:314) and is synonymous with *hettema* in v. 12. Likewise its opposite in v. 15 – *proslempsis* – means 'rise in rank' or 'acquisition' (see Josephus, *Antiquities* 17:17).

This theory has ethical implications which Paul hastens to bring home to the readers. It forbids any boasting on the side of Gentile Christians against unbelieving Jews. Contempt for people with a wrong or 'lower' religious identity is as a rule derived from a high opinion of the 'free will'. If it is a matter of your own decision whether you are spiritually on the right side (and consequently have God at your side) or not, then there is room for pride in yourself and contempt for others. In the Gospels this attitude is illustrated by the Pharisees' view of 'tax collectors and (other) sinners'. Paul has not denounced the self-complacency of a Jewish teacher of the Law (see Rom. 2:17–24) and a collective feeling of superiority of Israel as a chosen nation (see Rom. 3:27–30) in order to establish a Gentile Christian version of this same attitude. That is why in Rom. 11:16–14 Paul interrupts his teaching about Israel in order to convey this warning to his readers by means of an allegory taken from arboriculture.[49] He even seems to weaken the 'blessed assurance' that 'nothing can separate us from the love of God' (Rom. 8:38–39) when he warns those who pride themselves of having taken the place of Israel (11:19) that they in turn can be cut off from the roots of election in case they should fall away from faith (vv. 20–21). The assurance of faith should not be mixed up with a feeling of security that ignores the fact that the life of believers remains a journey and salvation is a process to be completed in the future (see 8:24–25).[50] This warning implies a big question mark with regard to large portions of Christianity, who, for a long time, have cultivated exactly this attitude towards Israel – the conviction of having replaced God's 'former' chosen people of Israel and having become the 'new' or 'true' Israel. God alone knows whether that is a reason why there were flourishing churches in some parts of the world which have been virtually 'cut off' from the tree of the Church. I wonder whether the lack of spiritual strength of the Church in many formerly 'Christian countries' may be God's answer to a

---

[49] It is disputed where exactly the apostle leaves the realm of rational arboriculture and constructs a development which does not occur in reality. In any case the text is not a parable in the stricter sense of the word but an allegory, i.e., a story with an artificial, improbable, or impossible content constructed merely to illustrate a message and not to demonstrate its plausibility.

[50] See 1 Cor. 10:12: 'So, if you think you are standing firm, be careful that you don't fall!'

self-complacency and illusive security that had taken possession of
many teachers and leaders of Christianity. In its context, Romans
11:17–24 is an aside.[51] Nevertheless, the message of this passage
may be one of the most relevant aspects of the theology of Romans
for our day.[52]

In Rom. 11:25 Paul adds another reason to his warning of unjus-
tified feelings of superiority over Israel. At the same time he is taking
up the thread of his argument in vv. 7–15. If the 'hardening' of Israel
served the end of spreading the Gospel to the Gentile world, then
there will be a time when this purpose has been sufficiently fulfilled.
That is what Paul is circumscribing in a somewhat vague manner
by the phrase literally translated by 'until the full measure of the
Gentiles has come in'. We do not know whether he is thinking of
a divinely limited *time* for the universal mission of the Church – or
for pagan dominance over Israel (see Luke 21:24?), or of a limited
number of Gentiles to be converted (see Acts 13:48), or of nations or
regions to be evangelised (see Rom. 15:19; Acts 13:46–47). In any
case, according to Rom. 11:25 the hardening of Israel is not only
partial (*ek merous*) from the beginning but also merely *temporary* so
that there will be a time when *all Israel* will understand the truth of
the Gospel – the true nature of God's 'righteousness' – and enjoy
that salvation which the Jews as yet fail to understand and accept
(see 10: 1–3).

There have been attempts to relate this prophecy to a new (spiritual or ecclesial) definition of the term 'Israel'. But this is excluded
by the opposition of 'partly' and 'all', and by the reference to the
previous 'hardening' of (the majority of) Israel (see v. 7). Paul is
speaking of a change in the status of Israel. This information would
not make sense if the meaning of the term 'Israel' were not the same
in the former and in the later context. There can be no legitimate
doubt that Paul is speaking of the historical, empirical, people of
Israel, both in his negative statements and in the positive ones. His
prophecy of salvation for 'all Israel' should be taken at face value,
i.e., as a confession of hope for Israel as a societal body (not necessarily pertinent to every single member of the nation at the time

---

[51] *Pace* Neil Elliott, *The Rhetoric of Romans* (1990).   [52] See below, ch. 9.

of its fulfilment). According to Acts 23:6; 24:24–26; 26:6–7; 28:20, Paul has confirmed this confession during his trial in Jerusalem and Caesarea not long after his writing to the Romans. There he interprets the resurrection of Jesus as the harbinger not only of the universal resurrection of the dead but also of a 'revival' of the chosen people (see prophetic promises such as Hos. 6:1–2; Ezek. 37:11–14; Isa. 25:8; 29:18; Dan. 12:1–2).

Paul's prophecy of salvation for Israel is introduced by the apostle in a very solemn way, as something about which readers should not be ignorant (see Rom. 1:13; 1 Thess. 4:13) and as a 'mystery' which transcends human wisdom. In other words, he is offering them a *revelation* (cf. Rom. 16:25). Nevertheless, he finds it attested in prophetic words from the Old Testament (taken mainly from Isa. 59:20 with an addition from Isa. 27:9). That is no contradiction, because Early Christianity was conscious of the fact that Jesus and the apostles detected new meanings in ancient Biblical texts. They were convinced that the Scriptures contained messages which had been concealed in former times in order to be revealed to the generation of the end (see 1 Cor. 10:11; 1 Pet. 1:10–12).[53]

As for the when and how of Israel's salvation, Paul's prophecy does not offer us a timetable or any other specification. As for the condition to be fulfilled, he continues to think in terms of some interrelationship between the history of the Gentiles and that of Israel (see vv. 12–15) but remains rather vague. As for the how, he does not speak of a conversion of Israel in response to the witness of the Church but – in the words of Isa. 59:20 – of a divine intervention by the coming 'redeemer'. While the prophet in all probability was thinking of God himself coming to redeem his people, the Early Christians did not expect a coming of God but the (second) coming of their Lord (see Rev. 2:25; 3:3, and texts with *parousia* such as 1 Cor. 15:23; 1 Thess. 2:19, etc.). In 1 Thess. 1:10 the expectation of Christ's coming is associated with the belief in His redeeming us from the impending final judgement. Similarly, in Rom. 11:26, the Scripture quotation promises a solution to the problem of godlessness and sin. Thus, Paul's teaching about the

---

53 See below, ch. 5.

salvation of Israel resembles his message of individual salvation by grace alone, although he is not using the terminology of justification in this context. The lack of any reference to faith is sometimes paralleled with the conversion of Paul himself, who was converted by an overwhelming revelation of the risen Lord in a way which leaves little room for the notion of a 'decision' for Christ and belief in a message.

So one day Israel will be saved, and Paul's prayers will be answered. A happy end and that's it? No, by no means. We should remember that Paul's concern was not only compassion with his compatriots but the question of God's faithfulness and the reliability of his word (see 9:6). Therefore, the goal of Rom. 9–11 has not yet been reached with the prophecy of Israel's salvation in v. 26, but only in the proclamation of the *basis* of this hope in v. 29: 'God's gifts and his call are irrevocable.' (Or, in the translation of J. B. Phillips, 'For once they are made, God does not withdraw his gifts or his calling.') This is not a logical deduction from a philosophical definition of God as unchanging and incapable of changing His mind. (In fact, the Bible does speak of several instances of God's changing His mind: see Gen. 6:6–7; Jonah 4:2.[54]) Rather, it is a confession of faith in God's promises as the decisive words of God which eventually will outweigh everything that speaks against their coming true. As an answer to the doubts concerning Israel's future, Paul could have quoted the oracle of Balaam on Israel from Num. 23:19: 'God is not a man, that he should lie, nor a son of man, that he should change his mind. Does he speak and then not act? Does he promise and then not fulfil?'

This assurance of God's faithfulness is the basis both of belief in the Gospel and of trusting the abiding election of Israel. No doubt, at present there is a tension between these two words of God: His calling of Israel, and His call to believe in Christ. The majority of Jews are enemies of the message that Paul is proclaiming (see 1 Thess. 2:15–16). But this attitude does not invalidate the love of God towards his people (see Rom. 11:28). After all, Paul is convinced that this – temporary – role of opposition to the Gospel has been

---

[54] See T. E. Fretheim, 'The Repentance of God. A Key to Evaluating Old Testament God-Talk', *HBT* 10 (1988), 47–70.

allotted to Israel by God Himself, see 11:7, 11–15. Obviously, the voice of God's love which speaks so powerfully through the death of Christ for our sins (see Rom. 5:8; 8:31–39) is not quenched by periods of error and alienation on the side of His people.

God's mercy as the mystery of history

This conclusion ends up in a reflection on the strange and un-predictable ways of God with His chosen people, on one hand, and the rest of humankind, on the other. There was a time when Israelites were the only people to whom the will of God had been revealed, so that they alone could steer clear of sin (see Gal. 2:15: non-Jews are sinners by definition). But with the coming of Christ and the proclamation of the Gospel things seem to have reversed: the majority of Jews did not respond to the Gospel, resisted the 'righteousness' of God as revealed in the Gospel, and failed to per-ceive its consistency with the previous revelation of God as attested in the Old Testament (see Rom. 10:1–4). However, this change of roles is not to be final since – strangely enough – it had been ar-ranged by God Himself. For what reason? In order to show mercy to all (see Rom. 11:30–32). The final message of the book of Jonah – God's compassion with all of His creatures – becomes the key to the meaning of all history, and this meaning turns out to be identi-cal with the meaning of the name of God as interpreted in Exod. 33:19 (quoted in Rom. 9:15): 'I will have mercy on whom I will have mercy, and I will have compassion on whom I will have compas-sion.' This result of Paul's reasoning (or this answer to his prayers) transcends our human notions of love. We can only think of love as an act of preferring some people while neglecting others. That is why the election of Israel and the election of believers in Christ (see Rom. 8:29–30:33) appear to us as mutually exclusive. Viewed from the end which Paul in Rom. 11 is teaching us to envisage, these two elections turn out to be complementary.

This conclusion leaves many questions unanswered. It is not the solution to all problems of soteriology and eschatology. But it is so amazing and comforting that it calls for a great confession of admiration for the wisdom behind the ways of God with this world of ours (see Rom. 11:33–36), partly quoted from Scripture

(Isa. 40:13 in v. 34, and Job 41:3 in v. 35). Its climax in v. 36 teaches that God is not only the source of everything (as a creator who has done his job and is now retired) but that He is also active in history and that He will be the consummation of all history. Thus, the 'doctrinal' part of Romans (chapters 1–11) ends with a doxology, which teaches us that all thinking about God should lead on to thanking God (see Rom. 1:20–21). The sequel in Rom. 12 will add the lesson that this gratitude calls for expressions beyond liturgy in a life that is dedicated to God in everything.

CHAPTER 5

Sorting the sources

In the previous chapters on major concerns of Paul in Romans we concentrated on the *contents* of this letter or on the *message* which the apostle tried to bring home to its readers. Our method consisted mainly in a close reading of what Paul is saying. Now we enter a different level of interpretation. Instead of simply tasting the dish, we try to find out its ingredients. By 'sources' we do not mean the innermost origins or reasons of his teaching in Romans (we shall not try to understand Paul better than he understood himself!), but the sources from which he draws his argument. Some of them may have been part of his earliest education in the home or in school (possibly under the eyes of Gamaliel the Elder, see Acts 22:3), before or after that time in Jerusalem also at Tarsus in Cilicia. Some traditions will have been transmitted to him when he joined the Church (though he attempts to downgrade the importance of such teaching in Gal. 1:12 – at least as far as the essence of the Gospel is concerned). But no doubt Paul continued to learn from the intellectual environment of his later ministry, from dialogue with the people he tried to win over to faith in Christ, and from conversations with converts in the various communities he founded or visited. To identify these inputs can contribute to a deeper understanding of the process of communication that is going on in this letter. In a way its recipients may have been co-authors of the letter – if Paul knew enough of their value system and general world view as well as of their specific Christian matrix, and if he paid tribute to it in order to convince them of what he wanted to communicate.

APPEAL TO AND INTERPRETATION OF SCRIPTURE

As early as in the second verse of the letter, the apostle indicates
that his message had a time-honoured background in the promises
of prophets that were laid down in Holy Scriptures. Therefore it
cannot come as a surprise that Paul refers to specific passages of
Scripture in several parts of Romans, either by explicit or tacit quotation, or by mere allusion. This feature of Romans deserves attention because there are letters of Paul with no scriptural quotations
at all (such as the Letters to the Philippians and the Thessalonians[1]) and others with considerably less frequent quotations (1 and
2 Cor.). Only the Letter to the Galatians (at least in chapters 3–5)
comes close to Romans in this respect. Obviously, this is due to the
doctrine of justification as the common topic of these two letters,
pointing back to at least *some* similarity between the situations in
which Paul wrote them.[2]

The fact that Rom. 1:2 refers to the prophets does not mean
that the quotations or allusions to Scripture are confined to the
prophetic books alone. Rather, it is an indication of the essential
assumption which governs Paul's use of Scripture – the conviction
that the Old Testament points to Christ and to the experience of
those who believe in him. This conviction is expressed at the end
of Paul's exegesis of Gen. 15:6 in Rom. 4:23–24, and as a general
principle in the conclusion of the whole letter-body in Rom. 15:4:
'For all the ancient scriptures were written for our own instruction,
in order that through the encouragement they give us we may
maintain our hope with fortitude' (New English Bible).[3]

A closer look at the distribution of quotations within the letter can
lead to additional insights. There are chapters in Romans with no
quotation at all (chapters 5, 6, and 16), and chapters with only one
quotation (see Rom. 1:17; 2:24; 7:7; 8:36; 13:9; 14:11). By contrast,
there are 'centres of gravity' in chapter 3:1–20; 4:9–11, and 15:1–
13. The main topics concerned are the message of justification by
faith alone and Paul's reflection about Israel.

---

[1] See E. Earle Ellis, *Paul's Use of the Old Testament* (Edinburgh and London: Oliver and Boyd,
    1957), appendix 1, 150–152.
[2] See above, in ch. 1.
[3] A similar statement of Paul's hermeneutical perspective is found in 1 Cor. 10:11.

In the question of the boundaries of the canon, Paul obviously shares the Pharisaic position (attested also by Josephus, *Contra Apionem* I 38–41), which later became normative. He appeals to texts from all three parts of the Hebrew Bible: Torah (in the narrower sense denoting the Pentateuch), prophetic books (including the narrative writings called 'earlier prophets' besides those books which bear the name of a prophet), and Ketubim - (other) writings (with the Book of Psalms as the most important part). Like most of us today, he seems to have his favourite books or passages, though at least in part for different reasons. Apart from subject-matter, which he preferred because it fitted into his argument or because he may have had his personal spiritual experience with it, it is very doubtful whether he possessed scrolls of all Biblical books. Thus, his predilections may have been influenced by circumstantial factors, but preferably we should try to understand them as a matter of deliberate choice from among a vast body of Biblical traditions which he knew and appreciated.

As for the Pentateuch, the apostle clearly concentrates on the Abraham tradition while showing little interest in Moses traditions (apart from quotations from the decalogue in Rom. 7:7 and 13:9). The whole chapter of Rom. 4 is dedicated to an exegesis of Gen. 15:6 ('Abraham believed the LORD and He credited it to him as righteousness'). This statement had been quoted already in Gal. 3:6, but there it did not carry the burden of proof. In Romans it is Paul's chief witness in his argument for justification on the basis of faith alone. But this understanding of the passage cannot be taken for granted. The apostle has to defend it against alternative readings of the Abraham tradition as a whole and of this verse in particular. No wonder that this fills a whole chapter! The figure of Abraham offered himself for the argument of Paul, whose concern was to defend his missionary principle of winning Gentiles for faith in Christ without an implicit or subsequent conversion to Judaism. Abraham had long since been considered as a model for Gentile converts to Judaism because he was born as a worshipper of pagan gods but 'discovered' God (by being called by him) or 'invented monotheism'. On the other hand, he knew nothing of the Law which was to be revealed through Moses, so that he could not be claimed as a model of a rigid observance of the Law.

However, he did receive the commandment to circumcise the male members of his family and household (though not a commission to spread this rite beyond this small community). In other words, the Abraham narrative was both a chance and a challenge to Paul in his attempt to justify his missionary practice as rooted in the Holy Scriptures.

It should be noted, however, that one chapter of Deuteronomy is also quoted several times in Romans. It is the 'Song of Moses' in Deut. 32, a text which was influential in Early Jewish eschatology (especially in those circles to whom only the Pentateuch was Holy Scripture in the stricter sense so that they could not base their hopes on prophetic books). The apostle quotes Deut. 32:21 in Rom. 10:19, Deut. 32:35 in Rom. 12:19, and Deut. 32:43 in Rom. 15:10. Taken together with quotations from Deut. 30 in Rom. 10:6–8 and Deut. 29:4 in Rom. 11:8, and an important allusion to Deut. 9:4 in Rom. 10:6, we come to the conclusion that Paul was ready to pay full tribute to the Torah proper, and that he found there sufficient support for his purposes.

As for the prophetic books, the book of Isaiah has been shown to be of higher importance for Paul's argument in Romans than for his earlier letters. It has been suggested that Paul studied this book for some time prior to his writing to the Romans. Paul quotes this prophet especially in support of his views on the relationship between Israel and the nations:

Isa. 52:5	in Rom. 2:24
Isa. 59:7–8	in Rom. 3:15–17
Isa. 10:22–23	in Rom. 9:27–28
Isa. 1:9	in Rom. 9:29
Isa. 8:14 and 28:16	in Rom. 9:33
Isa. 28:16 again	in Rom. 10:11
Isa. 52:7 (one of the roots of the notion of 'gospel')	in Rom. 10:15
Isa. 53:1	in Rom. 10:16
Isa. 65:1–2	in Rom. 10:20–21
Isa. 29:10	in Rom. 11:8
Isa. 59:20–21 and Isa. 27:9	in Rom. 11:26–27
Isa. 40:13	in Rom. 11:34–35
Isa. 11:10	in Rom. 15:12
Isa. 52:15	in Rom 15:21

This usage of Isaiah implies interpretations of his own calling in the context of world-wide mission (see especially Rom. 10:15–16; 15:21).[4] The chapters which modern research ascribes to an anonymous author (for convenience usually called Second Isaiah or Deutero-Isaiah) contain the usage of 'righteousness' as describing not the activities and character of a judge but of God as saviour (see Isa. 45:8; 46:13; 51:5; 56:1; 59:17), which is so characteristic of Romans (see Rom. 1:17; 3:21,22,25,26; 10:3). Another reason why Paul may have appreciated these chapters is the fact that Isa. 53 speaks of a vicarious death of a servant of the Lord – one of the rare Old Testament models for interpreting the death of Christ as a saving act of God predicted in Scripture (see 1 Cor. 15:3).

From the third part of the Hebrew canon, only the Book of Psalms contributes significant quotations to the Letter to the Romans. Its canonical status for Paul is attested to by his including such quotations under the heading *nomos* (Law) in Rom. 3:19. The preceding chain of quotations (3:10–18) has been chosen as a proof of universal sinfulness (including Israelites as the primary audience for which these texts were written). Likewise in Rom. 4:7–8 the quotation from Ps. 32:1–2 affirms the need for forgiveness, highlighted by the fact that it is King David who voices this confession. In a different context, the assumed Davidic origin of Biblical psalms is used as a vantage-point for putting them in the mouth of Christ as the 'Son of David'; see Rom. 15:3, 9–12.[5]

The actual wording of Paul's quotations from Scripture usually is in conformity with the majority text of the Septuagint. But there are cases of deviation, and for these several explanations are discussed: (a) casual mistakes due to quotation by memory; (b) intentional changes in order to fit the quotation into its Pauline context, e.g., to make it more effective for Paul's argument; and (c) wordings that are consciously closer to the Hebrew original than the Septuagint. This last explanation is discussed in two different

---

[4] According to Acts 13:47, it was especially in Isa. 49:6 where Paul could identify his own commission with the calling of the prophet to be 'a light for the gentiles' in order to bring 'salvation to the end of the earth'. In Paul's letters there is no quotation of this verse, but Gal. 1:15 seems to allude to Isa. 49:1.

[5] See Richard B. Hays, 'Christ Prays the Psalms: Paul's Use of an Early Christian Exegetical Convention', in *The Future of Christology. Essays in Honor of Leander E. Keck*, ed. A. J. Malherbe and W. A Meeks (Minneapolis, 1993), 122–136.

versions: the apostle who knew Hebrew and the Hebrew original of the text in question may have produced his own translation because the traditional Septuagint version seemed less suitable for his purposes. But he may also have used a revised version of the book from which he quoted. From the scroll of the Twelve Prophets discovered at Qumran, and from other traces in the manuscript tradition, we know that already in pre-Christian times – i.e., not as a reaction to Christian use of the Septuagint – a revision of the Septuagint had begun with the aim of bringing the Greek text nearer to the Hebrew original – a tendency which reached its climax in the new translation made by Aquila. In recent years the differences between New Testament quotations and our traditional editions of the Septuagint have been scrutinised more closely in order to distinguish between intentional changes and quotations from revised versions. This is a field for specialists, but the non-specialists should know at least that the case for postulating intentional changes has been weakened. Apart from choices within the range of possible readings, Paul and his contemporaries seem to have stuck closer to the accepted text of their Bible than former generations of scholars used to assume.

Some of Paul's interpretations of Old Testament passages sound strange to the modern mind, at least to those who have been trained to restrict the meaning of a text to that which its author wanted to communicate. But, if we compare Paul's exegesis with that of his Jewish contemporaries, his methods (though not his results!) turn out to remain within the range of possible and more or less plausible interpretation. In Romans we can identify typical examples of ancient exegetical rules which Jewish tradition attributed to Hillel (while, in fact, they were part of the general tools of Hellenistic philology). Thus, in Rom. 4:1–8 Paul combines Gen. 15:6 with Ps. 32:1–2 on the basis of the verb *logizomai*, which both texts have in common. This is an application of the rule called 'analogy' (*gezerah shavah*) by the Rabbis. At first glance it resembles our modern use of parallels for semantic purposes, but in reality it was used to clarify much more than the meaning of the word in question. The meaning of whole sentences was derived from one parallel, sometimes arbitrarily chosen. In the case of Rom. 4, the use of *logizomai* in Ps. 32:2 is in fact the closest parallel to that in

Gen. 15:6 – as far as the meaning of the verb itself is concerned. But the content of the quotation as a whole could easily serve as an argument against Paul's understanding of Gen. 15:6. (If God does *not* count *negative* actions, that does not exclude His counting or crediting good actions, including actions of faith.)

Another example from Romans of Paul's making use of conventional exegetical arguments is his comparison between Adam and Christ in Rom. 5:12–21. The phrase 'how much more' (*poso mallon*) in vv. 15 and 17 signals the logic called *qal wachomer* by the Rabbis: a conclusion from what is given (or 'easy') to what is to be proved (declared to be 'even more probable or plausible').

But not all rules to which Paul resorts are in conformity with the majority of ancient Jewish teachers. In Rom. 4: 9–11 he insists upon the fact that Abraham had been declared righteous (i.e., fully acceptable to God) before his being circumcised (because this rite was only introduced in Gen. 17). This argument from chronology or narrative sequel was advocated by Rabbi Aqiva in the early second century AD, but remained a minority position.[6]

EARLY JEWISH TRADITIONS

When buying a Bible today, we must decide whether or not it should include the apocrypha, i.e., the books contained in ancient manuscripts of the Greek Old Testament, but not in the Hebrew Bible. Some of them may have had a Hebrew original (like the wisdom book of Ben Sira or Ecclesiasticus), others not. In any case, they were never acknowledged as holy writings by the Jewish sages who fixed the boundaries of their Biblical canon in the first and second centuries of the Christian era. Thus, by the time of Paul, some Early Jewish writings were still candidates for canonicity which later on were excluded. Therefore it should not surprise us that in some passages Paul incorporates traditions attested in such early Jewish writings. For example, it has been observed that Paul's argument in Rom. 1:19–28 to a certain extent resembles a pattern that is elaborated more fully in the 'Wisdom of Solomon' (chapters 13–15) and which is also the background of the speeches in Acts 14:15–17 and

[6] See Sifre on Numbers § 131 on Num. 25:1.

17:24–28.[7] In addition, there is at least one instance where Paul introduces a quotation as if it were taken from the Old Testament but which cannot yet be identified with any extant writing, canonical or apocryphal (see 1 Cor. 2:9). On the whole, Paul seems to have restricted himself to the narrower canon which became normative in later Judaism and in the Protestant tradition. But that does not exclude the influence of a broader stream of Jewish traditions which had formed his mind and thereby contributed to his theology, including Romans.

A good example from Romans is the conjunction of the topics 'resurrection of the dead' and 'creation out of nothing' in Rom. 4:17, which echoes an encouragement for martyrdom in 2 Macc. 7:23, 28–29. Paul lifts these two topics to the level of essential markers of the identity of God. As for the first (resurrection of the dead), this is paralleled by the second of the Eighteen Benedictions (a very old part of the liturgy of synagogue service which may have existed already in Paul's days) and in the Hellenistic Jewish story of Joseph and Aseneth (20:7). This belief in the future resurrection of the dead forms part of the *Pharisaic* heritage of Paul.[8] The same can be said of Paul's insistence on *doing* what the Torah demands, instead of mere theoretical approval or even blatant hypocrisy (see Rom. 2:13, 17–29).

After the discovery of the Qumran scrolls, in 1947, all theories about the relationship between the New Testament and ancient Judaism had to be put to the test. Of course, this examination had to include the theology of Paul.[9] In view of Paul's Pharisaic background and of the differences (if not hostility) between Essenism and Pharisaism, there was no reason to expect revolutionary new insights. But in details the writings found in and around Qumran contributed to Pauline studies. The most remarkable example may be the attestation of the term 'works of the Law' and of the phrase 'count something as righteousness' in 4QMMT (= 4Q394–399),

[7] The list of quotations and allusions in Nestle-Aland's *Novum Testamentum Graece*, Appendix IV, lists ten points of contact between Romans and Wisdom. The *differences* between Wisdom and Romans are emphasised by E. E. Ellis, *Paul's Use of the Old Testament*, 77–80.
[8] See Acts 23:6–8.
[9] See e.g., J. Murphy-O'Connor, *Paul and Qumran. Studies in the New Testament* (Grand Rapids, 1972).

one of the writings which were published rather late after international protests against the delay of the editing process. These points of contact have helped the understanding of these expressions in Romans as part of a conventional Jewish terminology; but no essential affinity between Paul's message and the teachings of Qumran has come to light.

As early as in 1966, Henry Chadwick warned scholars not to expect too much progress in New Testament studies from the Qumran findings instead of drawing on the large bulk of Hellenistic Jewish literature.[10] In this field it is Flavius Josephus who provides priceless information about Jewish institutions, religious movements, and historical events of the century of the New Testament. As for theology, Philo of Alexandria is most perspicuous as a philosopher of religion and expositor of the Pentateuch. As speaker of a Jewish delegation sent to Caius Caligula, he must have been an old man or at least in a mature age when Paul was young. Although Paul's religious education under Gamaliel will have been more conservative than that of Philo, the fame of this learned man and creative thinker may have induced Paul to read some of his writings.

An acquaintance with Philo's thought might account for some similarities between Rom. 9–11 and passages in Philo's writings (unless these are due to similar conclusions drawn independently from common ground in Biblical texts). The first similarity is the downgrading of descent from the patriarchs in Rom. 9:6–13. A comparable (by no means identical) argument is found in Philo's *On Virtues*, 187–210 (especially in §§ 207–210) and in his tract *On Rewards and Punishments*, 58–60.[11] The difference between Paul and Philo lies in the decisive criterion which is moral quality in Philo,[12] but God's free choice in Romans. In their basic contention both authors are not affirming something which nobody would deny. According to Justin the Martyr in his *Dialogue with Trypho the Jew* (§ 140), there were Jewish teachers who trusted completely in descent from Abraham irrespective of conduct or faith.

Another, more peculiar, point of contact between Paul and Philo is their belief that proselytes may profit from a spiritual decline of

---

[10] See Henry Chadwick, 'St Paul and Philo of Alexandria', *BJRL* 48 (1966), 286–307, 286–7.

[11] See also *Praem. et poen.* 152.

[12] See the similar stance of John the Baptist in Matt. 3:7–10; Luke 3:7–9.

Israel. This teaching is implied in the allegory of the olive tree in
Rom. 11:17–24 and explicitly taught in its introduction in vv. 12–
15. It is paralleled in a passage near the end of *On Rewards and
Punishments* (§ 152), which is worth quoting in full:[13]

> The proselyte exalted aloft by his happy lot will be gazed at from all sides,
> marvelled at and held blessed by all for two things of highest excellence,
> that he came over to the camp of God and that he has won a prize best
> suited to his merits, a place in heaven firmly fixed, greater than words dare
> describe, while the nobly born who has falsified the sterling of his high
> lineage will be dragged right down and carried into Tartarus itself and
> profound darkness. Thus may all men seeing these examples be brought
> to a wiser mind and learn that God welcomes the virtue which springs
> from ignoble birth, that he takes no account of the roots but accepts the
> full-grown stem, because it has been changed from a weed into fruitfulness.

Not only the essential logic of the passage but also the imagery used
remind us of Rom. 11. The Biblical basis for both authors seems to
be Deut. 28:43–44:

> The alien who lives among you will rise above you higher and higher, but
> you will sink lower and lower. He will lend to you, but you will not lend
> to him. He will be the head, but you will be the tail.

This is one of the curses which are predicted to follow if Israel
should not live according to the rules of God's covenant (see Deut.
28: 15–68). Both Philo and Paul replace the foreigner who lives
among Israelites by the religious category proselyte or convert.
Philo keeps certainly nearer to the original meaning of the text in
concentrating on ethical values (though 'virtue' was a Hellenistic
term only rarely used in those books of the Septuagint which are
parts of the Hebrew canon), while Paul in the context of Romans
11 is deploring Israel's lack of faith and understanding (see Rom.
11:7, 20, 23, 25). But note that he nevertheless uses terms of moral
failure (see vv. 11 and 22).

So far the similarity between Rom. 11 and passages in Philo could
be explained as resulting from the Biblical basis of their thought. But
both authors go beyond that basis in the same direction when they

---

[13] The translation is taken from F. H. Colson, *Philo in Ten Volumes (and two supplementary volumes)*
(Cambridge, Mass., and London) (1939, repr. 1968), Vol. 8, p. 409.

teach that an end of the calamities for Israel will be the source of blessing to the other nations (and not the beginning of their decline as might be expected). In Rom. 11 this expectation is clearly stated in vv. 12 and 15:

If their stumbling brought wealth to the world and their loss meant wealth for the Gentiles, how much more will their restoration to fullness [add: be a blessing to the world].

For if their loss[14] has brought reconciliation to the world, what will their rise[15] bring about if not a change from death to life[16]?

The corresponding argument in Philo's writings is found in his *Life of Moses* 2:43–44:[17]

Thus the laws are shewn to be desirable and precious in the eyes of all, ordinary citizens and rulers alike, and that too though our nation has not prospered for many a year. It is but natural that when people are not flourishing their belongings to some degree are under a cloud. But, if a fresh start should be made to brighter prospects, how great a change for the better might we expect to see! I believe that each nation would abandon its peculiar ways, and, throwing overboard their ancestral customs, turn to honouring our laws alone. For, when the brightness of their shining is accompanied by national prosperity, it will darken the light of the others as the risen sun darkens the stars.[18]

These examples may teach us that not everything which is strange to us today sounded strange to Paul's contemporaries, and that not every alleged difference between Paul and Judaism is in contrast with all of ancient Judaism. Paul's conversion separated him from positions which had been essential for his previous religious career.

---

[14] There is no lexical justification for the widespread translation of *apobole* by 'rejection' (*pace* the erroneous reference to Josephus, *Antiquities* 4:314 in some dictionaries). The translation by '*amissio*' in the Vulgate is correct and had been retained by Luther's 'Verlust'. In any case, the term should be translated in a way which does not create a contradiction between Rom. 11:1 and Rom. 11:15.

[15] See H. G. Liddell and R. Scott, *A Greek-English lexicon, New Edition by H. S. Jones with the assistance of R. McKenzie and others, with a Supplement* (Oxford: Clarendon Press, 1968), 1519.

[16] It is a matter of dispute whether Paul is here speaking of resurrection metaphorically for a radical change for the better or teaching an eschatological conjunction of Israel's conversion as inaugurating the (general or first?) resurrection of the dead.

[17] Translation taken from Colson (see above, n. 13), Vol. 6, 469/471.

[18] That this is not only a theoretical reflection but a real expectation of Philo can be shown from *On Rewards and Punishments*, 163–172.

Alternative traditions of ancient Judaism may have helped him to find and formulate his new identity as a follower of Jesus and a Jewish messenger of the Gospel for the Gentile world.[19]

BASIC CHRISTIAN CONVICTIONS AND ECHOES FROM EARLY CHRISTIAN TRADITION

In this book we are primarily interested in the peculiar theological profile of Paul's Letter to the Romans. However, this concern should not seduce us into underestimating the importance of beliefs which Paul shared with more or less all Early Christians and which also play a role in Romans. Thus, the major titles of New Testament christology show up in adequate frequency and are at times consciously cumulated (see in 1:1–7; 5:1,11,21; 6:11, 23; 7:25; 8:39; 13:14; 15:30; 16.24).[20] As for the narrative tradition of the early Church, the death and resurrection of Jesus stand clearly in the centre, sometimes in conjunction as in the fundamental confession of 1 Cor. 15:3–4 (see Rom. 4:25; 6:3–10; 8:34; 14:9). Paul could speak of 'his gospel' as if he had a message of his own (see Rom. 2:16). But in 1 Cor. 15:11 he passionately protested against the idea that his message differed from that of the other apostles. While he was proud of pioneering as a missionary in regions untouched by previous evangelism (see Rom. 15:20–21), there is no evidence that he had an ambition to push theology towards new horizons (though he did just that according to widespread and well-founded opinion).

Pauline studies of the twentieth century have identified a number of (mostly short) passages in Paul's letters which the apostle did not compose but quotes from Early Christian tradition. In the case of 1 Cor. 11:23–25 (on the Lord's supper) and 15:3–5 (on Christ's death and resurrection as the centre of the Gospel) this is clear from the introductory formulas. All other cases are a matter of

[19] This may be true of points of contact with the school of Hillel such as a high esteem of baptism, the centrality of the love command, etc. which could be attributed to Paul's education by Gamaliel – as long as Gamaliel could be considered a member of this school, an error corrected by Jacob Neusner. See his *The Rabbinic Traditions about the Pharisees before 70* (Leiden, 1971), vol. 1, p. 295 and 376.

[20] The absence of 'Son of Man' is no exception because on the whole this phrase or title is not attested in early Christian confessions but restricted to the idiolect of Jesus as echoed in the Gospels.

conjecture. The reasons for assuming a fixed tradition were mainly formal (such as parallelism) and stylistic (especially the presence of vocabulary untypical of the apostle). The most famous example of such a theory is the so-called hymn in Phil. 2:6–11 ('so-called' because this designation has been questioned).[21]

In the Letter to the Romans, the following passages have been classified as such quotations of basic Christian texts: 1:3–4; 3:24–26; 4:25; 8:32(-34?); 10:9; 14:9.[22] Not all arguments for their isolation from the context and from Pauline authorship are compelling.[23] Especially when these alleged quotations are deemed too 'Jewish–Christian' to be Pauline, it may be asked which authority, apart from the evidence in his letters, can teach us how 'Jewish' Paul was. After all he emphasised his Jewish identity repeatedly (e.g., in Rom. 11:1). Besides, Rudolf Bultmann's verdict on Rom. 3:24 as non-Pauline was accompanied by outspoken objections against the 'mythical' doctrine of atonement by Christ's death, so that he seemed to feel happy that it was not 'distinctively Pauline' but 'only' traditional.[24] As far as I can see, scholars have become more cautious in reconstructing hypothetical sources or fixed traditions for form-critical reasons, partly because of methodological doubts, partly because of a shift of interest towards the author and his final product. In any case, supposed quotations should not be a reason to downgrade their content. Or should we assume that a preacher in his pulpit will quote a hymn which he does not like, just to please his parish folk?

BORROWINGS FROM SECULAR CULTURE

According to Acts 9:11; 21:39, and 22:3, Paul was a native of Tarsus in Cilicia, the administrative centre of a Roman province (where Cicero held office in 51–50 BCE). This very old city was a melting-pot of Greek and Oriental culture. Especially in the century of the

---

[21] See Charles J. Robbins, 'Rhetorical Structure of Philippians 2:6–11' *CBQ* 42 (1980), 73–82.

[22] I give the verse numbers without subdivisions which are relevant (or controversial) in some cases.

[23] See V. S. Poythress, 'Is Romans 1,3–4 a Pauline Confession After All?', *ET* 87 (1976), 180–183; N. H. Young, "Did St. Paul Compose Romans III:24f?', *ABR* 22 (1974), S. 23–32; C. E. B. Cranfield, *The Epistle to the Romans* I (Edinburgh: Clark 1975, 1985), p. 57 on Rom. 1:3–4 and p. 200 n. 1 on Rom. 3:24–25.

[24] See his *Theology of the New Testament*, vol. 1 (English trans. London: SCM, 1952), 295–96.

New Testament it was regarded as a centre of learning comparable
with Athens and Alexandria. No wonder that for several decades
Hellenistic influence had been held responsible for essential features of Paul's theology. The foundation of this view was shattered
by Willem Cornelis van Unnik in his study on Acts 22:3, *Tarsus
or Jerusalem? The City of Paul's Youth* (London, 1962),[25] which made
a convincing case for the assumption that according to Acts 22:3
Paul must have been still a child when he came under the influence of a conservative Jewish education in Jerusalem. Objections
against parts of the argument of van Unnik[26] do not disprove his
main result, that Acts 22:3 locates the whole formation of Paul's
personal identity in Jerusalem. On the other hand, his command
of the Greek language has been advanced as an argument against
the reliability of Acts 22:3. But young members of upper class
Jewish families (such as Paul's) could, and had to, learn Greek even
in Jerusalem. Apart from that, Luke's biography of the apostle includes a longer stay in Tarsus after Paul's conversion (see Acts 9:30;
11:25). He may have learned his trade as a tentmaker in these years
when his conversion had put an end to all aspirations of a career
within the Jewish establishment which his parents may have had in
mind. Thus, without questioning the result of van Unnik's investigation on Acts 22:3, we are free to imagine that Paul could and
did become familiar with Hellenistic culture as presented in the
city of Tarsus. But, contrary to earlier assumptions, this should not
be conceived of as part of the basis of his identity but rather as a
conscious encounter of a man of Jewish principles who had found
his calling within the Jesus movement with a special commission to
the Gentiles.

These biographical data justify the expectation that the letters of
Paul are not only informed by Jewish traditions and Early Christian
beliefs but also by a considerable amount of secular learning on a
level above the average of ancient Mediterranean population. This
can be ascertained above all by Paul's making use of rhetorical
devices – a fact which has received fresh attention in the past

[25] See above in ch. 1.2.
[26] It may be questioned whether the participles 'brought up' (*anatethrammenos*) and 'educated' (*pepaideumenos*) refer to clearly distinct phases.

twenty-five years.[27] As early as in his thesis of 1910, Rudolf Bultmann had studied similarities between the style of Paul's letters and a type of didactic dialogue of ancient philosophers called *diatribe*.[28] Other studies have revealed Paul's familiarity with conventions of ancient letter-writing which were a topic of education and learned discussions. (His modifications of, or deviations from, such conventions, as in Rom 1:1–7, turn out all the more telling.)

While these matters may be regarded as merely formal, there are also examples of terms and topics of theological reflection in Romans which cannot be traced back to Old Testament and Early Jewish sources but can be explained as echoes of Greek philosophy, however loosely applied. For example, the conjunction of Law and nature (*nomos* and *physis*) in Rom. 2.14, or of law and reason (*nomos* and *nous*) in Rom. 7:23, 25, reminds us of reflections in Greek philosophy without being dependent upon them. A clearer case of a borrowing from a philosophical tradition is Paul's use of the term 'the inner human being' in Rom. 7:22. This concept (though not the exact wording) originated in Plato (see *Resp.* 9.589a). Its emergence in 2 Cor. 4:16 points to a specific context where it became relevant. No doubt, Paul integrates it into his general theological convictions. But it also contributes to a clarification of his views and inaugurates lines of anthropological thinking which became influential in later developments.[29] The fact that Paul does not use the term consistently but for rather different purposes in two rather different contexts illustrates that he will have regarded such Hellenistic philosophical traditions as servants, not authorities for his thinking.

A very popular notion of classical antiquity which Paul integrates into his theology is the comparison of a society or group with a

---

[27] This has been highlighted by several contributions to the volumes on *The Romans Debate*, edited Karl P. Donfried (original edn, Minneapolis, 1977, revised and expanded edn. Peabody, 1991).

[28] See Rudolf Bultmann, *Der Stil der paulinischen Predigt und die kynisch-stoische Diatribe* (Göttingen: Vandenhoeck and Ruprecht, 1910). The state of the art in this field, as far as Romans is concerned, is presented by S. K. Stowers, *The Diatribe and Paul's Letter to the Romans* (Chico, 1981), and by his article 'Paul's Dialogue with a Fellow Jew in Romans 3:1-9', *CBQ* 46 (1984), 707–722.

[29] See Hans Dieter Betz, 'The Concept of the "Inner Human Being" (ὁ ἔσω ἄνθρωπος) in the Anthropology of Paul', *NTS* 46 (2000), 315–341.

body. It has entered into our speaking of an 'organisation' with its 'members'. Paul uses this metaphor for the Church in 1 Cor. 12:12–27 and Rom. 12:3–8 in order to argue for the equal dignity of each function in the Church. The roots of this view are in Greek philosophy (see Plato, *Resp.* 462c.d and Chrysippos, fragm. 367), but it is also well attested in Jewish[30] and Roman[31] writings before and after Paul's making use of it. The most famous example of its rhetorical impact is the story of Agrippa Menenius Lanatus, who, according to Livy, *Ab urbe condita* II 32:8–12, used it successfully in order to win over the rebellious plebeians for renewed co-operation with the patricians in the year 494 BCE.

This example opens the door for a closer look at points of contact between Paul's Letter to the Romans and concepts or catchwords that were particularly popular in Roman society at the time of its composition. So far, this horizon of Romans has not yet been sufficiently taken into account. Perhaps it can bring some fresh air into a scene where too many people think that they have already heard or read everything that has been said and that has to be said on the subject. Therefore it may be permitted to devote a full chapter to this rarely trodden avenue.

---

[30] See Philo, *De specialibus legibus* III:131; Josephus, *Bell. Iud.* I. 507; II: 264; IV:406.
[31] See Seneca, *Ep. Mor.* XVII.102:6; Curtius Rufus, *Historia Alexandri Magni Macedonis* X 9:1–4.

CHAPTER 6

To the Romans a Roman? The rhetoric of Romans as a model for preaching the Gospel in Rome

ROMANS AS A DOCUMENT OF MISSIOLOGY AND THE IDEA OF CONTEXTUALISATION

In the last decades the exegesis of Romans has moved away from a doctrinal interpretation, which took Paul's teaching as timeless truth without asking to whom and for what he was writing. Instead, attention has focused on the letter's purpose(s) in the context of Paul's missionary work. Some commentators have specified this in *apologetic* terms: large portions of the letter can be read as a defence of the Gospel which Paul has been proclaiming in previous years. He had met opposition against his course of receiving Gentiles into the Church without requiring them to accept Jewish ritual traditions. In his letter to the churches of Galatia, he had been fighting fiercely against agitators who tried to win over Gentile-Christians as converts to Judaism. The Letter to the Romans has much in common with the Letter to the Galatians. It is therefore reasonable to assume that in Romans Paul is continuing this discussion about the principles of evangelism among people of non-Jewish origin. His impending visit to Jerusalem may have increased the urgency of additional arguments for his case. Surely this is one of the reasons why we find so much reflection on 'Jews and Greeks' in the Letter to the Romans.

On the other hand, some scholars have cautioned us against neglecting the real addressees of the letter. In Rom. 15 the visit to Jerusalem is mentioned because it is the last obligation which Paul feels he must fulfil before his visit to Rome, which he had planned and awaited for so many years. Both in chapter 1 and in chapter 15 Paul emphasises his heartfelt desire to come to Rome in order to serve the believers there. Moreover, he hopes to make Rome his starting-point for a new and adventurous outreach to the West. Therefore, it is necessary to read the letter more in the context of the *future* which Paul envisages than in the context of memories of past conflicts. While there is some truth in reading Romans as Paul's 'testament' (many others have written down their will in situations of crisis only to continue their journey for a couple of years!), there is *more* truth in understanding Romans as a manifesto declaring the principles of missionary preaching which Paul intends to apply when coming to Rome. To convince the Roman believers of these principles was all the more important for Paul because he hoped to receive their support for his outreach towards Spain, the Western 'end of the world' according to the ancient Mediterranean world view.

Those who emphasise this background of the letter usually think in terms of the necessity for Paul to appeal to common traditions of Early Christianity as the basis of agreement and harmony. However, only relatively few examples of this strategy can be identified with certainty (see chapter 5). They are scattered within the large body of this letter and contribute little to the distinctive features of Romans if compared with other Pauline letters. What is more characteristic of Romans is the amount of new ideas in Paul's argument – be it in his use of Scripture (as in chapters 4 and 9–11) or in his appeal to human experience (as in chapter 7). This innovative force of the letter's content should be related to the apostle's pressing forward to new horizons of his missionary work – in Rome and beyond, in the more Romanised parts of the empire.

Certain peculiarities of Romans suggest a reflection along the lines of modern concepts of mission that have been developed in connection with the ecumenical movement. Parallel to the spread of political independence among former colonies, many churches that had been founded and shaped by European or North American missionaries discovered that they had been estranged from their national culture or tribal traditions. They felt the need of an 'indigenous theology' resulting from an encounter between the Biblical message and those cultural traditions. While ultimately this means a task to be performed by the recipients themselves, the essential insight implies a challenge to missionaries to go as far as they can towards a dialogue with the culture of the peoples and places of their respective mission fields. The most widespread catchword for this missionary strategy is *contextualisation*. Can it be applied to Early Christian missionary activities?

Yes and no! Or rather 'No and yes'? As far as the New Testament is concerned, all our documents are written in Greek and come from the Mediterranean world, politically from within the Roman empire, culturally from regions that had been more or less Hellenised for three hundred years.[1] Nevertheless, there was considerable cultural variety, especially in connection with the variety of traditional languages as a vehicle of regional traditions. As early as in the original Church of Jerusalem, we find 'Hebrews' alongside 'Hellenists' (Greek-speaking Jews), and Stephen's skilful use of Old Testament traditions may reflect a 'wisdom' that had been cultivated more in Alexandria than in Jerusalem (see Acts 6:5, 10; 7:2–53). As for Paul, he seems to have been familiar with both milieus: he can proudly call himself a 'Hebrew (born) from Hebrews' (whose command of the 'Hebrew' = Aramaic language is attested by Acts 21:40; 22:2), but he also debates with Hellenists (see Acts 9:29) and writes letters in a style that is well above the colloquial Greek of his day. Was he not an ideal candidate for the task of building bridges across cultural barriers in the service of the Gospel?

But was it his concern? Was he conscious of the problems of cross-cultural communication? Was he not convinced that one Gospel was enough for the whole world, regardless of differences of nationality, gender, and social status (see Rom. 3:29–30; 1 Cor. 12:13; Gal. 3:28)? True. And yet there is one clear testimony of Paul's accommodating his missionary strategy to the respective character of the target groups of his witness. In 1 Cor. 9:20–22 he writes:

To the Jews I became like a Jew, to win the Jews. To those under the law I became like one under the law (though I myself am not under the law), so as to win those under the law. To those not having the law I became like one not having the law (though I am not free from God's law but am

---

[1] Contrary to theories from the early twentieth century, this includes the Jewish homeland; see Martin Hengel in collaboration with Christoph Markschies, *The 'Hellenization' of Judaea in the First Century after Christ* (London: SCM Press/Philadelphia: Trinity Press International, 1989).

under Christ's law), so as to win those not having the law. To the weak I became weak, to win the weak. I have become all things to all men so that by all possible means I might save some.

One might object that the difference between Jews living accord-ing the Law and Gentiles (not knowing this Law, see Rom. 2:14) is a religious or theological one and not a cultural one. But note that this contrast is only the beginning and that Paul goes on to generalise the principle of his conduct ('all things to all men . . . by all possible means'). That Paul could apply this principle to very special local settings was the conviction of at least one au-thor, who must have known more of Paul than all we epigones:[2] In Acts 17:22–31 Luke depicts Paul as answering brilliantly to the cu-riosity of some Athenian 'philosophers', alluding to some of their intellectual traditions and to their contempt of popular religion without denying essentials of the Biblical message (which in fact turned out as stumbling-blocks at least to parts of the audience). This story shows that contextualisation as a term is a modern in-vention, but that the idea behind it could be conceived of already by some Early Christians. Can it account for certain peculiar features of Paul's Letter to the Romans? A comparison between several traits of Romans and secular sources on contemporary Roman culture and ideology yields some results which I consider to be noteworthy.[3]

PEACE IN ROMANS AND IN ROMAN PROPAGANDA AND RELIGION

In chapter 4 I had described the prominent place of the idea of peace (with God and in human relations) in various parts of the Letter to the Romans. This emphasis is paralleled by the frequency and importance of this topic in Roman sources, both literary and

---

[2] Of course, I know of colleagues who are confident that they *understand* Paul better than Luke did. But that cannot be discussed here. It does not affect the lesson to be learned from the example.

[3] The topic of this chapter has been anticipated more than a hundred years ago in a short contribution to the *Expository Times* which drew attention to elements of Roman law as the background of several passages of Romans; see Edward Hicks, 'A Roman to Romans', *ET* 5 (1893/94), 565–567; and 6 (1894/95), 93–94. Since then there has been very little reflection along this line (as far as I know).

epigraphic ones (inscriptions and coins).[4] To be more precise, the popularity of the idea of peace was the result of the career of Augustus and of the establishment of the principate after decades of civil unrest and civil war. The most perspicuous expression of this background was the erection of an altar for the veneration of the 'Peace of Augustus' (*ara pacis augustae*), dedicated in the year 9 BCE . But already Caesar had been praised as 'peacemaker' in the funeral oration of Mark Antony,[5] perhaps an echo of coins with *pax* inscriptions minted by Caesar towards the end of his life. The theme was amply developed by poets of the Augustan age such as Ovid,[6] Tibullus,[7] and Virgil.[8]

What is less known, this praise of the 'Roman peace', established and guarded by the Julio-Claudian dynasty, had a second heyday in the years when Paul wrote to the Romans. Late in the year AD 54 a promising young ruler named Nero Claudius Caesar Augustus Germanicus succeeded his stepfather (Claudius), who had become rather unpopular in the course of his reign. At the time of his access to power Nero was hardly 17 years old, and within a year the people understood that this new ruler had no ambition to achieve military victories. Instead he showed himself eager to promote cultural events and to please the public himself with poetry and other performances as an artist. Unfortunately, in his attempt to appear as the greatest pop-star of his age, he overestimated his own talent. But initially he was greeted by the public with great enthusiasm. Among his predecessors, he preferred Augustus as the example he promised to follow.[9] We have several literary works in which the final consummation of peace on earth is ascribed to him or expected from him. A poet from Sicily named Calpurnius sings:[10]

The unholy War-Goddess [Bellona] shall yield and have her vanquished hands bound behind her back, and, stripped of weapons, turn her furious teeth into her own entrails; upon herself shall she wage civil wars which

---

[4] See Stefan Weinstock, 'Pax and the "Ara pacis" ', *JRS* 50 (1960), 44–58, and plates V–IX.
[5] See Dio Cassius, *Roman History* 44:49, 2.   [6] See *Fastii* I 711–12.
[7] See *Elegies*, I 10:69–70.   [8] See his famous fourth eclogue and in *Aen.* 6:851–853.
[9] See Weinstock, 'Pax and the "Ara pacis" ', 51.
[10] Lines from *Eclogue*, 1:46–67, abridged and translated by Neil Elliott, 'Romans 13:1–7 in the Context of Imperial Propaganda', in *Paul and Empire. Religion and Power in Roman Imperial Society*, ed. Richard A. Horsley (Harrisburgh, 1997), 184–204, 202.

of late she spread o'er all the world . . . Fair peace shall come, fair not in visage alone . . . Clemency has commanded every vice[11] that wears the disguise of peace to betake itself afar: she has broken every maddened sword-blade . . . Peace in her fullness shall come; knowing not the drawn sword, she shall renew once more the reign of Saturn[12] in Latium, once more the reign of Numa who first taught the tasks of peace to armies that rejoiced in slaughter.

Similarly an anonymous poet of the same time, whose verses have been discovered in the library of the Swiss monastery of Einsiedeln, wrote (*Eclogue* 2: 25–31):

We reap with no sword, nor do towns in fast-closed walls prepare unutterable war: there is not any woman who . . . gives birth to an enemy. Unarmed our youth can dig the fields, and the boy, trained to the slow-moving plow, marvels at the sword hanging in the abode of his fathers.[13]

In his fourth eclogue, lines 142–146, Calpurnius overtly ascribes the achievement of this peace to Nero and shows himself convinced that he must be one of the gods, disguised as a man (possibly Jupiter himself!). In a similar vein Seneca's nephew, Lucanus, composed an introduction to his epic on the civil war in which he anticipates the deification of Nero in connection with the universal end of all wars.[14]

If Paul shows a predilection for the language of peace (and harmony) in his Letter to the Romans (and not in other letters), the most natural explanation is that he was consciously alluding to this ideology. That does not mean that he was willing to subscribe to the claim that peace on earth was the gift of the rulers of the empire. Far from that, his verdict on them is probably implied in his quotation from Isa. 59:8 in Rom. 3:17: 'They do not know the way of peace.' (In the tradition of Biblical language this means not only ignorance but lack of concern and experience.) What made this phraseology of peace attractive for Paul's interpretation of the Gospel was its obvious appeal to the public, which indicated a deep longing for

[11] Perhaps an allusion to the tract *De clementia* which Nero's tutor Seneca dedicated to him shortly after his enthronement.
[12] That is the golden age. [13] Translation see n. 10.
[14] See *Pharsalia*, I: 44–47 and 60–62.

peace among ordinary people. After all, there had been too much bloodshed in the last decades of the republic and during the rise of Octavian/Augustus to power. On the other hand, to emphasise the peace dimension of the Gospel was in no wise misleading. Paul had the backing of his favourite prophet (Isaiah) for this choice (see Isa. 52:7, quoted but abridged in Rom. 10:15 and alluded to in Acts 10:36 and Eph. 2:17).

But what about peace *with God* or *reconciliation* with Him? Of course, this terminology for the centre of his message used in Rom. 5:1, 10, 11 has no parallels in the imperial propaganda. But it does answer to a deep concern of traditional Roman religion. While Greek philosophy increasingly repudiated the idea that gods are subject to moods and that men must fear their wrath, the concern for peace with the gods (*pax deorum* or *pax deum*) was a vital issue for conservative Romans.[15] Disasters of their history were interpreted as divine judgements and called for efforts to implore the peace with the gods.[16] Thus, Paul is taking advantage of a happy coincidence when he introduces the Gospel which he intends to preach in Rome as focusing on the problem of God's rightful wrath (see Rom. 1:18) which is overcome by Christ's atoning death (see Rom. 5:9–11) in order to bestow peace with God on all believers through our Lord Jesus Christ (see Rom. 5:1). While the apostle does not hesitate to denounce pagan polytheism and worship of creatures (certainly including rulers) instead of the creator, he does not despise points of contact which can serve as bridges for future converts on their way to faith in Christ.

To sum up, both the interpretation of the Gospel and the emphasis on peace and harmony in ethical passages of Romans can be understood as a conscious tribute to values of the cultural context of the addressees. In introducing himself to the Roman Christians, Paul is not only displaying his 'orthodoxy' in terms of Early Christian convictions and his faithfulness to the heritage of the Old Testament, but also his creative capacities in encountering new horizons of missionary endeavours.

---

[15] Certainly not for rationalists such as Lucretius; see his *De rerum natura* V 1224–1232.
[16] See Livy, *Ab urbe condita* III 5:17; 7:7; 8:1.

RIGHTEOUSNESS (OR, JUSTICE) AS ROMAN BENEFIT AND AS GOD'S ACTIVITY, GIFT, AND CALLING

Ever since Martin Luther and his fellow-reformers, the interpretation of Paul's Letter to the Romans has emphasised the doctrine of justification and of God's saving righteousness as its major concern. To include this topic in this chapter on *distinctive* ideas of Romans may astonish those who still believe that Paul is teaching this doctrine in every letter. But it also risks objections from those who know that justification is a common topic of Romans and Galatians! While the heat of the conflict in the earlier letter marks a difference between Galatians and Romans,[17] the discussion about the Law and circumcision is continued, and some scriptural arguments from Galatians return in Romans, though modified. Nevertheless, a look at word statistics will teach us that the topic of righteousness or justice plays a much greater role in Romans than in Galatians. As a matter of fact, it is only the verb *dikaioo* which links both letters (used 15 times in Romans and 8 times in Galatians). As for the noun *dikaiosyne* the frequency leaps from 7 in Galatians to 34 in Romans; for the adjective *dikaios* from 1 to 7; and five additional words from this family do not occur in Galatians but only in Romans (*dikaioma* 3 times, *dikaiosis* twice, and *dikaiokrisia* once, *adikia* 7 times and *adikos* once). The relative length of Romans cannot sufficiently explain these numbers. The evidence points to a palpable shift of perspective.

This impression is strengthened when we consider the places where the pertinent words appear in the structure of the letter. Already the so-called motto or proposition of the letter contains both the noun and the adjective: 'In the gospel God's righteousness is revealed . . . the righteous will live by faith' (1:17). This is the message which Paul has to preach to Greeks and non-Greeks (1:14), and which he is not ashamed of because it offers salvation to Jews and non-Jews (1:16). It is the message he hopes to proclaim in Rome in the near future (1:15), so we may suspect that he is clothing it

---

[17] After all, Paul could speak to the Galatians as a father while he was a stranger to most of the believers in Rome.

in words which he intends to use when he has arrived there. Then follow some instances where the need of salvation is shown to be caused by human unrighteousness (see Rom. 1:18, 29; 2:8; 3:5). When the apostle returns to the positive content of the Gospel there is again a cluster of words from this root (see 3:21–26, 28, 30). The same is true of Romans 9:30 – 10:10. All these texts trace the (gracious) justification of believers back to the righteousness of God. And all of them emphasise the *universal* scope of this saving activity of God in Christ.

Now let us for a moment deprive this vocabulary of its specific theological meaning but keep the basic structure (righteousness/justice for the whole world). What we get is another central idea of Roman pride and propaganda. The tradition of associating Roman culture with righteousness is even older than the ideology of peace in that it dates back to the times of the Roman republic. And, contrary to the case with peace, there is evidence that Paul even shared this high esteem of the Roman legal institutions and the spirit behind them. In his plea for loyalty to the existing political order (i.e., to Roman dominance over the Mediterranean world) in Rom. 13:1–7, he argues not only on a theological level (teaching that world history is under God's control so that the ruling powers have to be accepted, see vv. 1–2) but also on a pragmatic level (submission is safer because of the punitive power of the state, and active cooperation is even more promising in view of possible rewards, see vv. 3–5). To underline this reference to jurisdiction, Paul reminds the readers that this is also the legitimate reason for their paying taxes (v. 6).[18] More precisely, he is speaking of *tributes* (*phoroi*) which had to be paid by the members of subdued nations, not by Roman citizens.[19] This is an echo of a widespread pattern of argument used by Roman officials in order to praise the benefits

[18] The *gar* (for) at the beginning of the sentence shows that this verse is not yet an exhortation to pay taxes (such as follows in v. 7), but a statement of facts which confirm the opinion voiced in v. 5.

[19] That is why Paul, as a Roman citizen, says 'you' and not 'we' in this statement. This is the only hint at his civil status in his letters, and a rather tacit one. If the difference between slaves and free citizens had become irrelevant in Paul's eyes (see Gal. 3:28), then his Roman citizenship deserved no attention in his correspondence with fellow believers. The exception in Rom. 13 is due to the topic 'tribute'.

of Roman dominance and to justify the material cost of accepting the Roman rule.[20] Apparently Paul has no objections to admitting at least a kernel of truth in this claim, and we in turn should be rather slow to criticise him in this respect: is not the heritage of Roman law in our legal traditions in fact the most valuable part of the legacy of the Roman culture?

Of course, this political application of the Roman claim to an extraordinary talent for justice is not the root of the tradition. It could even be questioned by self-critical Romans as Tacitus does by quoting a certain Calgacus, leader of a Britannic rebellion against Roman dominance in AD 83.[21] On a philosophical level, the idea of righteousness is an essential part of the idea of humanism (*humanitas*) which was coined by the Romans, not yet the Greeks.[22] At the same time, it is claimed as a notable part of the national character of the Romans. While Cicero quotes this conviction ironically in order to criticise a questionable economic policy of the Roman state,[23] Valerius Maximus, in the thirties of the first century, asserts that 'among all nations our society is the outstanding and clearest example' of righteousness.[24] According to Cicero, righteousness, together with peacefulness, was part of the legacy of the legendary Roman King Numa Pompilius.[25]

In view of this well-attested, widespread, and long-lived tradition, the peculiar emphasis on righteousness in Paul's Letter to the Romans cannot be haphazard. The apostle must have been blind and deaf if he had not noticed the popularity and importance of the idea of righteousness in Roman circles (which he certainly had met

---

[20] See Cicero, *Ad Quintum fratrem* I 1:34–35; Velleius Paterculus, *Hist. Rom.* II 117:3; Tacitus, *Hist* IV 73–74; Aelius Aristides, *Or.* XXVI *(On Rome)* 67; Cassius Dio, *Hist. Rom.* LII 29; Orosius, *Hist. Adv. Pag.* V 1:10–12.

[21] See Tacitus, *Agricola* 31:1–2: *Works, Vol. I, Agricola*, trans. M. Hutton, rev. R. M. Ogilvie (Cambridge, Mass.: Harvard University Press, 1970): 'Our goods and chattels go for tribute; our lands and harvests in requisitions of grain; life and limb themselves are worn out in making roads through marsh and forest to the accompaniment of gibes and blows. Slaves born to slavery are sold once and for all and are fed by their masters free of cost; but Britain pays a daily price for her own enslavement, and feeds the slavers, . . . '

[22] See Cicero, *De legibus* I 10:28 (Human beings are 'born for righteousness') and *De finibus bonorum et malorum* V 22:65.

[23] See *De re publica* III 9:16.   [24] See *Facta et dicta memorabilia* 6:5.

[25] See *De re publica* I 14:26. A later Christian writer of antiquity, Minucius Felix (*Octavius* 25:1–2), confronts this 'very famous and noble Roman righteousness' with the sagas about crimes and vices in the very cradle of the new-born Roman state.

in cities like Philippi, Ephesus, and above all Corinth). To make such ample use of the pertinent vocabulary exactly in his letter to Rome must have been a conscious decision resulting from homiletic (or hermeneutic) reflection. Again, as with the topic of peace, this strategy will have implied a dialectical approach. Paul could whole-heartedly join hands with the moralists who proclaimed the ethical principle of righteousness (see Rom. 6:13, 16, 19–20; 14:17). At the same time, he was certainly determined to question the pride of Roman society and to confront it with the gap between theory and practice (see 1:18–32; 13:12–13). Especially he would have preached the Living God as the only personification of *true* righteousness, and the Gospel as the message of righteousness for all the world. In fact, it sounds like an echo of the Letter to the Romans when in the late first century 'letter of Clement' (in reality a letter of the church of Rome to the church of Corinth) we read that Paul, 'having been a herald in the East and in the West . . . taught righteousness to the whole world'.[26]

But what about the risk of misunderstanding the Christian message because of the lack of congruence between the semantics of *dikaiosyne* in the Biblical tradition and in secular philosophical traditions?[27] Was there any chance to convey the affinity between righteousness and mercy in the Old Testament (which was at the basis of Paul's concept of the 'righteousness of God') to a Roman audience? No doubt the Greek tradition of understanding righteousness as giving everyone his due (reward *or punishment*) could create serious obstacles for the communication of Paul's message of justification.[28] However, there is evidence of remarkable differences between Greek and Roman concepts of righteousness. In *De republica* III 7:10–11 Cicero explicitly criticises 'the majority of philosophers, especially Plato and Aristotle' for their definition of righteousness which virtually reduces this virtue to a quality of judges and rulers instead of attributing it (in principle) to all human

---

[26] See 1 Clem. 5:7. The same letter may also have been influenced by Paul's emphasis in Romans on peace and harmony. Its main objective is to help the Christians of Corinth to overcome tensions and strife in their ranks. See 1 Clem. 20:10–11; 60:4; 61:1; 62:2; 63:2; 65:1 especially with Rom. 16:17–20.

[27] See above in ch. 4, pp. 53–54.

[28] Even Martin Luther had to wrestle with this problem; see below pp. 154–155.

beings irrespective of social class. In III 15:24 he goes on to ascribe to 'righteousness' the connotations of 'forbearance with everybody and a concern for the welfare of the human race'.[29] Another aspect of the Roman understanding of righteousness which lent a hand to Paul's purposes was its association with the important Roman ideal of *faithfulness* (*fides*, translated by *pistis* in Greek texts but not identical in its meaning[30]). Cicero (in *De officiis* I 7:23) could write: 'The basis of righteousness is faithfulness (*fundamentum autem est iustitiae fides*)' – a sentence which Paul could have quoted with approval while giving it a fresh meaning!

This is not the only example of Latin texts with a conjunction of terms which Paul could use as points of contact for the communication of the Gospel. In *Rep.* III 17:27 Cicero praises a man of 'highest *righteousness*, singular *faithfulness*' (*summa iustitia, singulari fide*). Another significant combination is between *peace and justice* as in verses of Ovid which glorify the merits of Augustus (*Metam.* XV 832–833). According to Seneca (*De clementia* III 17:8 (or I 19:8)) ideal conditions under a good ruler include justice and peace – benefits which even the provinces enjoy if only they accept their Roman overlords (see Tacitus, *Hist.* IV 74:1). There are even instances where peace, righteousness, and faithfulness occur together. According to Petronius (famous for his satirical *Banquet of Trimalchio*), the three goddesses *Pax, Fides,* and *Iustitia* fled when the civil war between Caesar and Pompey began (see *Sat.* 124: 247–253). A panegyric of Velleius Paterculus on Tiberius makes faithfulness and righteousness return and discord flee under the reign of this monarch (see *Hist. Rom.* II 126:2). Is it by chance that one of the rare instances with 'the kingdom of God' in Paul's letters – Rom. 14:17 – speaks of 'righteousness, peace and joy' as its essence?

LIMITS OF THE LAW AS OF LAWS IN GENERAL

A striking phenomenon which cannot easily be explained from Jewish traditions is the series of negative verdicts on the Law of Moses or on laws in general in several chapters of Romans. Some

---

[29] '*parcere omnibus, consulere generi hominum*'.
[30] In one place at least – Rom. 14:23 – Paul seems to use *pistis* in the sense of the Roman 'good faith' (= 'honest intention' or 'good conscience').

of these statements are anticipated already in Galatians, but in a more casual way and less unequivocally, so that it is legitimate to discuss them in this chapter on characteristic features of Romans. The points in question are the following:

(a) Contrary to Jewish theories about a pre-existence of the Law, Paul insists on the plain meaning of the Old Testament tradition according to which the Law was given to Moses at Mount Sinai after the exodus from Egypt – centuries after the beginnings of God's history with a chosen family, the ancestors of the people of Israel (see Gal. 3:17; Rom. 5:13–14, 20). To Paul (and his contemporaries), this late date of the legislation through Moses is no mere matter of chronology, since in antiquity chronological priority as a rule suggested superiority.[31] The lesson that Paul wants to bring home to his audience was that the *promises* given to Abraham and his descendants (including his spiritual 'descendants', the imitators of his faith) were of far greater importance than the requirements of the Law.

(b) According to Rom. 3:19–20 and 4:15, the essential function of laws is to reveal, condemn, and punish transgressions. This is also the meaning of the phrase 'curse of the Law' in Gal. 3:13 – which is sometimes misunderstood as if it declared the Law to *be* a curse[32] – and of Gal. 3:19. Although this function of laws (and of the Law) is necessary and politically positive, it speaks strongly against assigning too much weight to observance of the Law in the context of salvation.

(c) In a number of passages in Romans Paul goes a step further in constructing a still more negative connection between the Law and sin. According to Rom. 5:20, the later addition (or should we translate 'intrusion'?) of the Law had the *aim* of increasing or multiplying transgressions! The same idea is hinted at in Rom. 4:15; 6:14; and 7:5–6 (possibly already in Gal. 3:19). Then it is explicitly developed in Rom. 7:7–11:

I would not have known what sin was except through the Law. For I would not have known what coveting really was if the Law had not said 'Do not covet.' But sin, seizing the opportunity afforded by the commandment,

---

[31] This is the main reason for all claims of pre-existence; see John 1:15.
[32] For this clarification see Gal. 3:10.

Gen 3
allusion

produced in me every kind of covetous desire. For apart from law, sin is dead. Once I was alive apart from law; but when the commandment came, sin sprang to life and I died. I found that the very commandment that was intended to serve life actually brought death. For sin, seizing the opportunity afforded by the commandment, deceived me, and through the commandment put me to death.[33]

To be sure, this passage contains some striking parallels to the story of the Fall in Gen. 3. But to read this story as an anticipation of the impact of the Law on human behaviour must have sounded outrageous to Jewish ears – and that may be one reason why Paul does not explicitly quote or refer to Gen. 3. But what else could have secured the plausibility of his story? Could the readers of Romans follow the argument of the apostle in this passage? What was strange and shocking for readers with a Jewish background may have been familiar to people brought up in and surrounded by a pagan environment. Let us consider these three stratagems to downgrade the Law from a Roman perspective:

(a) As for the later date of the Law, we find the idea of a 'Golden Age' without laws in several sources. Seneca (*Letters* XIV 90:6) ascribes it to the stoic philosopher Poseidonios. Its popularity in Rome is attested by a passage in Ovid's *Metamorphoses* (I 89–92) and (later) by Tacitus (*Ann.* 3:26) in a critical comment on the flood of new laws promulgated under Tiberius (possibly an echo of contemporary discussions).

(b) That laws must include regulations for the punishment of transgressors is presupposed already by Plato (see in his *Laws* IX 853c; 854c.d; 870e; 871a). Therefore Philo felt obliged to give an explanation of the fact that the decalogue does not end with such penal laws. Roman authors shared this definition of 'law' as imposing sanctions on transgressors (see Cicero, *Rep.* III 11:18 and Seneca, *Letters* XV 94:38).

(c) The striking idea of Paul that the Law not only fails but that specific commandments are likely to induce people to transgress them is paralleled in writings of Cicero and Seneca. In a speech in court (*Pro M. Tullio* 9), Cicero claims that murder had been very rare in the times of the ancestors. That is why they had no

---

[33] Translation from the New International Version, slightly modified.

law against bandits. In his opinion, to enact a law against a crime which did not yet exist could have encouraged people to commit it.[34] More important, because published shortly before Paul's Letter to the Romans, is a passage in Seneca's writing *De clementia* (I 23:1) which he wrote as an instruction and (hopeful) programme for his former pupil, now young emperor, Nero. Seneca mentions the frequency of capital punishment for patricide under Claudius and goes on to say: 'As long as there had been no law against this crime, only very few children dared to commit it . . . patricide started with the law, and the penalty showed them the crime.' Apart from these texts from juridical contexts, there is ample evidence from Roman sources which teaches that the psychological analysis contained in Rom. 7:7–11 was in no wise new to the readers of Romans. It had been propagated by Publilius Syrus, a very popular actor and writer of proverbs of the first century BCE who was widely read in late antiquity and the Middle Ages.[35] It is also well attested in the erotic poems of Ovid. The closest parallels to Rom. 7:7–11 are in his *Amores* III poem 4:9, 11, 17, 25, 31: 'Stop arousing vices by forbidding . . . '.[36] According to Tacitus (*Ann.* XIII 12:2; 13:1), it was this principle which made a woman named Acne more attractive for Nero than his legitimate wife, Octavia, and which frustrated the reproaches of Nero's mother against this liaison.

To round out the picture, it is worth mentioning in this context that the continuation in Rom. 7, especially vv. 15–20, recalls the mythical figure of Medea, who killed her sons from Jason because he had deserted her. According to Euripides, she knew that she would commit a terrible crime but could not resist her violent feelings.[37] The popularity of this story in Rome is attested by the fact that both Ovid and Seneca produced Latin versions of the play. The inner conflict before the bloody act had been put in paintings by artists (e.g., in Pompeii and Herculaneum). This leads us to the next topic of our soundings in the Roman context of the Letter to the Romans.

---

[34] A similar argument is found in Cicero's speech *Pro domo sua*, 49:127.
[35] See the saying in his *Sententiae* N 17: 'Desire loves nothing more than what is forbidden.'
[36] See also ibid. II 19:3.   [37] See Euripides, *Medea* 1077b–1080.

THE POWER AND UNIVERSALITY OF SIN

Romans 7 is only the climax of a line of argument which runs through the early chapters of this letter and which betrays what may be labelled as Paul's ethical (or anthropological) *pessimism*. He is not content with referring to the fact that sins occur from time to time and then forgiveness is needed (and offered by God). His message of *universal* salvation in Christ implied that the threat was as universal as the comfort (or in the favourite terms of the 'new perspective on Paul': the 'plight' as universal as the 'solution'). The apostle argues this case in Rom. 1:18–3:20, beginning with a sombre picture of mankind's religious failure and subsequent moral decline – a picture that he could paint with the colours of traditional Jewish polemics against the pagan world (see 1:18–32). But then he goes on to question the assumed superiority of Jews who overestimated their knowledge of God's will as revealed in the Law and overlooked their shortcomings in living according to the Law. While in Rom. 2:17–29 this is no general reproach against all Jews, the quotations from Scripture which follow in 3:9–19 are adduced as proof that Jews are no less sinners than pagans. The conclusion is drawn in 3:22–23: 'There is not difference [i.e., between Jews and Gentiles], for all have sinned and fail to give glory to God.' At this point of the argument, this insight has been derived from Scripture. In Rom. 7 it will be confirmed by experience. The best that the Law can achieve is to convince our minds; but it cannot really control our actions which are ruled by irrational forces.

We are used to thinking that this strong emphasis on human sinfulness is beyond the natural capacities of human introspection, that it has to be revealed and to be believed. On the exegetical level we have been taught that Paul himself had never lived the conflict which he describes in Rom. 7, but that this chapter is his analysis of human existence from a post-conversion viewpoint. Therefore, it comes as a surprise that we can find the same harsh verdicts on human sinfulness as in Romans in writings of Seneca:

We all have sinned [*peccavimus omnes*], some more, some less, some with determination, some by accident or induced by the depravity of others. Some of us had good intentions but lacked the firmness to stick to them

Sin & Seneca's writings which is a collection of ideas following anthropological reflection

and lost their innocence against their will and resistance.[38] And we did not only fail in the past but will continue to do so until the end of our lives. (*De clementia* I 6:3)

Not one will be found who can absolve himself, though everybody calls himself innocent – in view of what witnesses can prove, not what conscience knows. (*De ira* I 14:3)

If we want to judge everything justly, we must start by persuading ourselves that nobody of us is without guilt . . . Who is it who can declare himself innocent with regard to all laws? And even if that be the case – how poor is such an innocence: to be good according to the law! The field of duties is much larger than the requirement of law! . . . But we cannot even guarantee our compliance with this artificial definition of innocence: some things we performed, some we planned, some we wished, some we indulged; at times we are innocent because something did not work. (Ibid. II 28:1–3)

Human nature produces deceitful characters, ungrateful ones, covetous ones, impious ones. When you have to judge the behaviour of one individual, consider what is common. (Ibid. II 31:5)

Even the most prudent fail. (Ibid. III 25:2)

So let us come to an end [sc. after a long series of lamentations] lest guilt be attached to our century. Our ancestors deplored this, we deplore it and our posterity will deplore it: that morality has been destroyed, iniquity reigns, human affairs become worse and worse . . . It is always the same what we have to proclaim about ourselves; we are wicked, we have been wicked and, I do not like to add: we shall be wicked. (*De beneficiis* I 10:1, 3)

You are wrong, my dear Lucilius, if you think that extravagance and neglect of good manners and whatever everybody blames his times for are a vice of our century. This is not a matter of times but of men: no generation has been void of guilt. (*Ep. Mor.* XVI 97:1)

Now why this long litany? To show that these are not casual remarks but expressions of a real concern of the philosopher, products of anthropological reflection. And since Seneca had been more a collector than an inventor of ideas, we can read his writings as witnesses of the kind of thinking that was 'in the air' among educated

[38] See Rom. 7:14–23.

people of Rome in the middle of the first century. Without assuming that Paul had read Seneca (although he had met his brother Gallio in Corinth, see Acts 18), we can imagine that Paul had a feeling for this atmosphere of ethical pessimism and that he was confident of winning approval with verdicts that are less popular in our times.

That Paul really did share special traditions with Seneca can be verified in the case of the idea of *conscience*. Many years ago Krister Stendahl protested against reading Luther and Augustine back into the letters of Paul.[39] The truth in his case was that Paul did not yet know that relentless search for selfish motives behind such innocent behaviour as a baby's cry for milk. Nor did he question the purity of religious zeal if it did not include the willingness to be bound for hell if that were God's will. But to speak of Paul's 'robust conscience' creates a misleading impression. As a matter of fact, our very idea of conscience (as judging our past actions *and ruling our decisions for future actions*) was just emerging at the time of Paul – and the apostle shared this development. It is a development in which Roman authors seem to have gone beyond their Greek teachers. Especially the use of the term in Rom. 13:5, where conscience serves as moral authority *independent of societal sanctions*, is in line with frequent statements in Latin literature.[40] Again, the most impressive evidence comes from the writings of Seneca, who, although primarily in a Stoic tradition, recommended the practice introduced by Epicurus to scrutinise one's conscience every evening. A striking convergence with Paul can be observed when Seneca gives conscience a religious dimension:

A god is near to you, with you, in you. Yes, I say, my Lucilius, a holy spirit has his seat in us, an observer and guardian of our bad or good (actions). He deals with us as we deal with him. Indeed, nobody is a good man without (the help of) a god . . . In every single good man '*lives a god, though which god, is uncertain*'." (*Ep. Mor.* IV 41:1–2).[41]

---

[39] See his essay 'The Apostle Paul and the Introspective Conscience of the West' in *HThR* 56 (1963), 199–215.

[40] See Cicero, *Milo* 83; Velleius Paterculus, *Hist. Rom.* II 115; Seneca, *Vit. Beat.* 20:4; *Ira* III 41:1; *Benef.* VI 42:2.

[41] The quotation within the quotation is from Virgil, *Aeneis* 8:352.

Replace the polytheistic, generic 'god' with the Biblical name 'God', and you arrive at something very near to Rom. 2:15–16.[42] And there you can see from the closing of v. 16 ('according to my gospel') that Paul invested this notion of conscience with the highest possible importance – probably because in the life of Gentiles it played the part which the Torah played in that of Jews (see v. 14).

So what? Did Paul simply share such ideas as a part of the education he had received? As 'a Hebrew of Hebrews'? To me that strains our historical imagination too much. Instead, I suggest that he kept learning from every milieu in which he lived and proclaimed the Gospel, and that his thinking was increasingly moving towards Rome while he was planning to go there with increasing impatience.

A ROMAN PATTERN OF `NOBLE DEATH´ ECHOED IN ROMANS?

In recent years, attention of New Testament scholars has been drawn to the notion of 'noble death' in ancient pagan sources.[43] While the traditions about Jewish martyrs from the second century BCE had been taken into account in earlier studies concerning the meaning of Christ's death, these recent studies have broadened our horizon. The very stories about Jewish resistance against the Hellenisation of Jewish religion in 2 and 4 Maccabees turned out to have been influenced by Hellenistic thought-modes. They share the concept of noble death – 'noble' because of the reasons for dying and for the way it was accepted and endured.

In Romans 5:7 Paul alludes to cases of voluntary death on behalf of a righteous person or of persons who deserve such a sacrifice. He goes on to demonstrate the extraordinary quality of Christ's death in that he died for people who did not deserve such a benefit but were sinners and enemies of God. By contrast, according to John 15:13, 'there is no greater love than this – that a man should lay

[42] Especially if in v. 16 you accept the reading of Codex Vaticanus and my translation of *hemera* as meaning 'court' (as in 1 Cor. 4:3).
[43] See especially David Seeley, *The Noble Death. Graeco-Roman Martyrology and Paul's Concept of Salvation* (Sheffield: JSOT Press, 1990).

down his life for his *friends*'. Paul's conclusion in Rom. 5:8 is that God's love in Christ surpasses all human examples of 'noble death'.

As far as I can see, a specific *Roman* version of 'noble death' has not yet received sufficient attention in the interpretation of Romans. It should be considered as a possible background of Rom. 9:3, where the apostle refers to his readiness to sacrifice himself on behalf of his fellow-Israelites. It is not quite clear whether he speaks of a mere wish or a prayer or even a vow he once made. The content of this wish or vow was to become a 'dedication' (*anathema*) for his people. This term can mean either something dedicated for cultic purposes, for example, in temples or something devoted to evil, dedicated for destruction. In the letters of Paul, only the second meaning is attested (see 1 Cor. 12:3; 16:22; Gal. 1:8). Therefore, it is universally acknowledged that in Rom. 9:3 Paul is offering either his life or even his own salvation as a vicarious sacrifice for the salvation of Israel (see Rom. 10:1). The wording of this wish or vow recalls the Roman term for solemn sacrifices of military leaders on behalf of their armies (and the nation): *devotio*. Especially three successive members of the family of the *Decii* were renowned for having performed this sacrifice in desperate situations in order to secure the support of the gods in favour of their compatriots.[44] The act included a ritual of self-dedication before the commander rushed forward in order to seek death by the hands of the enemy.[45] The popularity of this tradition is attested by numerous allusions in Roman literature before Paul's Letter to the Romans,[46] and by his contemporaries Seneca, Lucanus, and Pliny[47] as well as by later authors.[48] Cicero could compare his own role as consul (when he merely risked his life without losing it in his fight against Catilina) with the heroism of the Decii.[49]

---

[44] See Livy, *Ab urbe condita* VIII 6:9ff and 10:26ff.

[45] See descriptions given by Cicero in *De Natura deorum* II 10; *De divinatione* I 51 and Seneca in *Ep. Mor.* VII 67:9.

[46] See *Rhetorica ad Herennium* IV 44:57; Cicero, *De finibus* 2:61; *Pro C. Rabirio Postumo* 2; *Tusc. Disp.*1:89; Livy, *Ab urbe condita* IX 4:10; Manilius, *Astronomica* I 789; Valerius Maximus, V 6:6.

[47] See Seneca, *De beneficiis* VI 36:2; Lucanus, *Bell. Civ.* II 312–313; Pliny the Elder, *Nat. Hist.* 22:9; 28:12.

[48] See Minucius Felix, *Octavius* 7.3; Ammianus Marcellinus, XVI 10.3; Augustine, *De Civitate Dei* 5.18.

[49] See his speech *Pro domo sua* 24:64/65:65.

To be sure, Paul, as a pious Jew, was familiar with other models of sacrifice on behalf of the nation when he uttered the prayer or made the vow mentioned in Rom. 9:3. As a former zealot he must have known and cherished the example of the heroes of the Maccabean revolution whose deaths had been interpreted as sacrifices for the benefit of the people (see 2 Macc. 7:37–38; 4 Macc. 6:27–29 and 17:21–22). But that does not exclude the possibility that in Rom. 9:3 he chose a wording that would appeal to Roman ears.[50]

The memories of Maccabean martyrdom are also discussed as a possible background for the interpretation of the saving death of Christ in Rom. 3:24–26. The alternative interpretation – that *hilasterion* in Rom. 3:25 is an allusion to the *kapporet* or 'mercy seat' of Lev. 16 and, hence, to the feast of atonement – suffers from the weakness that it is doubtful whether readers of Romans had sufficient insider knowledge about rituals from *first* temple times to be able to understand this allusion.[51] While the general idea of atonement through sacrifice was certainly rooted in cultic performances, the application of this idea to the death of martyrs was not fixed to a specific sacrifice. As a model for the interpretation of Christ's death, the traditions about human martyrdom offered a nearer analogy than sacrifices of animals in a former ritual of old Israel. Having detected a convergence of Jewish and Roman traditions about martyrdom on behalf of the nation, the case for assuming this background for Rom. 3:24–26 has been strengthened. It is worth noting that the idea of *redemption* (*apolytrosis*) of the nation *through the blood* of a dying hero is also attested in connection with the Roman *devotio*. In a dialogue between Brutus and Cato (Uticensis), Lucanus makes Cato allude to Decius and reflect his own impending death with the words: 'May my blood *redeem* the commonwealth, may my death be a propitiation for whatever

[50] Jan Willem van Henten, *The Maccabean Martyrs as Saviours of the Jewish People. A Study of 2 and 4 Maccabees* (Leiden, 1997), 146–151, 208–9, describes this Roman tradition and quotes some of the relevant texts. He even discusses the possibility that already the Maccabean martyrdom stories might have been influenced by the Roman *devotio*. (Note: there had been diplomatic contacts between the Maccabees and the Romans! See 1 Macc. 8 and 12:1–4:16; 14:16–19, 24).

[51] The original *kapporet* of the first temple had been removed by the Babylonians and as far as we know there was no substitute in the second temple.

punishment the degeneration of Rome may deserve.'[52] Likewise, Seneca asks his friend Lucilius:

> If circumstances demand that you die for your country and *pay* with your own salvation for the salvation of all citizens – will you be ready to offer your neck willingly, not reluctantly?[53]

Even the idea of peace with the gods restored by the *devotio* of the Decii is discussed by Cicero.[54]

To sum up: Paul certainly did not *need* pagan models in order to develop the idea of sacrificial death. But the Roman tradition starting from the rite of the *devotio* of military leaders was so popular that it could serve as a model for communicating this part of the Gospel of Christ in a Roman environment. Rom. 9:3 comes even closer to this Roman tradition because Paul offers himself as a sacrifice for *his nation*. Thus, there is reason to assume that Paul knew this tradition and was willing to exploit it in the course of his intended preaching in Rome.

With the evidence presented in this chapter I hope to have made a case for the presence in Romans of a hermeneutical strategy at least similar to the modern idea of contextualisation. While the essential attitude behind it is attested in 1 Cor. 9:20–23, it could not be taken for granted that it was applicable to the cultural differences of local milieus and to the different profiles of Pauline letters. In recent years there have been several studies of local milieus as reflected in New Testament letters. I expect that such studies will confirm and correct each other and in the long run will contribute to a more dynamic picture of New Testament theology as a process of communication in time and space.

---

[52] See *Bell. Civ.* II 308–313.   [53] See *Ep. Mor.* IX 76:27.
[54] See *De natura deorum* III 15.

CHAPTER 7

Romans in its canonical context

ROMANS AMONG THE LETTERS OF PAUL

Comparisons of Romans with other Pauline letters can be under-taken from different aspects. A popular aspect is to look for devel-opments of Paul's theological outlook. Thus, various topics of Paul's teaching, such as eschatology, have been traced through the collec-tion of his letters in order to interpret the differences as evidence of certain tendencies. To some scholars, Romans has appeared as the climax or consummation of Paul's theology, while others have preferred to read it as a document of compromise or even of retractation.

All these theories are highly dependent upon premises concern-ing chronology and authorship which are not universally agreed. The designation of Romans as a 'testament' of Paul evokes the notion that this is the latest of Paul's letters (although this is no necessary implication of the term 'testament': a sense of crisis can be sufficient reason for someone to write down a testament – and then to live on for many years!). As a matter of fact, the quality of a 'final account' of the apostle emerges only on the basis of (a) a minimalist position in the question of authorship (accepting only Romans, 1 and 2 Corinthians, Galatians, Philippians, 1 Thessalo-nians, and Philemon as authentic Pauline letters); and (b) a decision on Philippians which rules out Caesarea maritima and Rome as possible places of composition. The former presupposition has been widespread in continental European scholarship but continues to be disputed on the international scene. The latter has the consen-sus of centuries against it and seems to lose its plausibility in recent

years (not only in the English-speaking world).[1] This uncertainty of
the case of Philippians affects such important topics as individual
eschatology (see Phil. 1:23), or Paul's attitude towards Judaism (see
Phil. 3:2–9).[2]

The auspices for determining the place of Romans in the course
of developments in Paul's thinking are weakened even more if we
give some letters with disputed authorship a chance of Pauline
authorship or indirect Pauline origin. Especially letters from prison,
such as Colossians, Ephesians, and 2 Timothy, are candidates for a
composition not by but *on behalf of* the apostle whose liberty to dictate
letters may have been restricted by unfavourable circumstances.

In view of these uncertain variables and the unstable status of
relevant studies, it would seem unwise to propose a specific theory
on the place of Romans in an overall development of Paul's theology. Instead I am going to draw attention to several aspects which
allow us to group Romans together with other letters of Paul's as
they stand (the so-called *Corpus Paulinum*).

The close similarity between Romans and Galatians has been
touched upon earlier.[3] It is almost universally agreed that Romans
was written after Galatians, but the time span between the two
letters is disputed. Many exegetes regard the close similarities as
such as sufficient proof for assuming a date not very much earlier
than that of Romans. But this is by no means compelling, since
earlier discussions can 'boil up' after some time when comparable
circumstances recur. Thus the impending journey to Jerusalem,
rumours of the situation in Judea, and fresh indications of Jewish
enmity against Paul's missionary work may have prompted Paul to
continue the discussion which he had begun in Galatians.[4] As for
the evidence in Galatians itself and in relevant passages of the Acts
of the Apostles, there is a growing tendency to prefer the 'South
Galatian' localisation of the Galatian congregations which allows
a much earlier date of the letter than the 'North Galatian' theory
(without demanding it).[5]

---

[1] See Gerald F. Hawthorne, *Philippians* (Waco: Word Books, 1983).

[2] In addition, critical judgements which cut Phil. 3 out of the frame of this letter result
in complete agnosticism as for the date of this alleged fragment of a different Pauline
letter – another obstacle for any theory of a development in this matter.

[3] Above all, see in ch. 4.   [4] See above, ch. 1.

[5] See James D. G. Dunn, *The Theology of Paul's Letter to the Galatians* (Cambridge: Cambridge
University Press, 1993), 12–17.

A comparison between the *theology* of Romans and that of Galatians reveals a shift of emphasis in the interpretation of their common topic (the message of justification by faith alone on the basis of the atoning death of Christ). In Galatians, the apostle does not speak of peace or reconciliation in this context. Instead the aspect of *freedom* is central in Galatians (see Gal. 2:4; 4:21–31; 5:1, 13), while in Romans it is present but less important (see Rom. 6:18, 22; 8:2, 21). That Jesus died on a cross is emphasised in Galatians (see Gal. 3:1 [,14]; 5:11; 6:12,14), while in Romans it is only implied in the wording of Rom. 6:6, an ethical teaching in line with Gal. 5:24. In Galatians, the inferiority of the Law is demonstrated above all by its later date as compared with the promises given to Abraham (which are interpreted as an anticipation of the Gospel), and by its only temporary function (see Gal. 3:15–4:6), while in Romans Paul stresses the limited or even negative effects of the Law (see Rom. 3:20; 4:15; 5:13, 20; 7:5, 7–11; 8:3). Above all, in Galatians Paul's attitude towards Judaism (or rather the Judaists as representatives of an aggressive version of Judaism) is rather hostile (see Gal. 4:21–31; 5:12)[6] while in Romans Jewish opposition against Paul's missionary work is mentioned without polemical comments (see Rom. 11:28; 15:31). A hope for Israel as the people of God may be implied in Gal. 6:16, but the wording is by no means clear, while in Romans a major part of the letter is devoted to this concern (chapters 9–11). In my opinion, these changes of style, mood, and content can be better explained by the assumption of a longer time interval between these two letters. In addition it must be taken into account that the Galatian churches had been founded by Paul, while the Christian groups in Rome were quite independent of his previous work but, in his mind, candidates for co-operation which he wanted to win.

Another difference between Romans and Galatians, but also between Romans and the Corinthian correspondence, is the way in which Paul speaks of his apostolic office. In Romans it is almost exclusively a topic of the frame of the letter, not of the letter-body (see Rom. 1:1, 5; 11:13; 15:15–21) and apparently it is no controversial issue. By contrast, in Gal. 1:1,11–24; 2:1–10 Paul has to defend his apostolic authority by pointing out his being called by a direct

---

[6] A link between Galatians and 1 Thess. 2:14–16 that fits well into theories of an early date of both epistles.

revelation from God and his recognition by the mother Church of Jerusalem. The Corinthians, too, must be reminded of his vision of the Risen Lord as the basis of his calling (see 1 Cor. 9:1; 15:8–10). Later on, some members of the Corinthian Church developed an idea of apostleship which other preachers seemed to represent in a more impressive manner. In 2 Cor. 10–12 Paul responds to this challenge by making a virtue (or rather, a grace) of his bodily weakness, while insisting on the fact that his service had not been void of proofs of his divine commission such as miracles wrought through him (see 2 Cor. 12:12).

Apart from that, the letters to the Corinthians are truly 'pastoral' letters which (partly on request) discuss a wide range of doctrinal and ethical problems that have emerged in the community. Paul's writing to the Thessalonians belongs to this genre, too. In Romans, only the exhortations of the 'strong' and the 'weak' in chapters 14–15 share this character (if, indeed, they address existing problems and not simply dangers which the apostle knew from his experience with the Corinthians).

In Paul's Letter to the Philippians, the passage on justification instead of self-righteousness in chapter 3:2–11 is a close parallel to teachings in Romans. But the polemical tone seems to connect it more with Galatians. However, this change of atmosphere could be the result of the troubles which the apostle had to face in Judea soon after he had written to the Romans (if the letter was written from Caesarea or Rome).[7] There he had to learn that the majority of Jewish-Christians were fervent defenders of the Law, and in their attitude towards him were influenced by slanders issuing from hostile Jews (see Acts 21:20–21). Another shift of emphasis from Romans to Philippians may be seen in Phil. 3:20–21, where Paul declares the irrelevance of all earthly citizenship and transfers the title of 'Saviour' – in the ancient world a widely used attribute for political benefactors – to the Lord, whose return from heaven believers urgently await.

Among the letters of the Pauline collection with uncertain authorship, that to the Ephesians echoes the central message of Romans in Eph. 2:8–10.[8] Also the sequel in Eph. 2:11–22 breathes

---

[7] See Acts 21–26.

[8] For a closer comparison, cf. I. Howard Marshall, 'Salvation, Grace and Works in the Later Writings in the Pauline Corpus', *NTS* 42 (1996), 339–358, esp. 342–348.

the spirit of Romans with its emphasis on peace between Gentiles and Jews. The passage could easily be read as a continuation of Romans 15:1–13. However, the praise of Paul's ministry in Eph. 3:1–13 resembles strongly the final doxology of Romans (16:25–27), which is regarded as a later addition by the vast majority of commentators.

An echo of Rom. 1:3–4 can be seen in 2 Tim. 2:8: 'Remember Jesus Christ, raised from the dead, descended from David.' However, the similarity does not necessarily result from imitation since it is based on a reading of 2 Sam. 7:12, which may have influenced other New Testament passages, too (see Acts 2:30–32; 13:23–37). The Pauline antithesis of grace and works recurs in an abstract of the Gospel in 2 Tim. 1:9–10 and in Tit. 3:3–7.[9]

ROMANS AND OTHER LETTERS OF THE NEW TESTAMENT

The first epistle of Peter shares Paul's message of the grace of God as the basis of salvation (see 1 Pet. 1:10, 13; 3:7; 5:10, 12) and the source of gifts in the church (see 1 Pet. 4:10). But it lacks the distinctively Pauline contrast between grace and works (of the Law). The closest connection between Romans and 1 Peter concerns the Christian attitude towards the political world (see Rom. 13:1–7 with 1 Pet. 2:13–17). The similarity consists in the conviction that the institutions of the state have to punish the wicked and to reward benefactors. The reference to tribute and taxes of Rom. 13:6–7 is lacking in 1 Peter, while the warning of a misunderstanding of Christian freedom is a surplus in 1 Pet. 2:16. The case for a common tradition is stronger than that for any dependence between the two passages.[10] Recent studies on 1 Peter have dismissed older theories of a Pauline influence on 1 Peter (sometimes connected with the name of Silvanus, who is mentioned in 1 Pet. 5:12 and has been identified with Silas of Acts).[11]

A famous and time-honoured conundrum of Biblical theology is the tension between James 2:14–26 and the Pauline teaching on

---

[9] See ibid., 348–354.
[10] For a detailed comparison, see E. G. Selwyn, *The First Epistle of St Peter* (London: Macmillan, 1949), 426–429.
[11] See e.g., J. H. Elliott, *A Home for the Homeless. A Sociological Exegesis of 1 Peter, its Situation and Strategy* (Philadelphia, 1981).

justification.[12] Both authors appeal to Gen. 15:6 and the justification of Abraham as their fundamental model of righteousness
by faith. However, James regards faith and works as complementary conditions of salvation, while Paul insists on faith as the sole
presupposition on Abraham's part for his being declared righteous.

The dominant tradition in modern exegesis has been to read
James 2:14–26 as a protest against the theology of Paul as displayed
in Galatians and Romans. Alternatively, the 'enemy' or target group
of James has been identified as radical adherents of Pauline theology who went beyond the apostle in downgrading the Law and
were less sensitive to the ethical risks of a full-blown Christian anti-
nomism. However, the trend of recent studies on James is to be
more reluctant with reading James in comparison with Paul.[13] The
argument of James 2:19 ('Even the demons believe') presupposes
a rather superficial idea of faith, which only beginners or learners
may have erroneously nourished. Thus, the warning not to neglect
the practical, active, and ethical aspect of Christianity could be
addressed to converts without any polemics against a theological
position which proclaims what James is rejecting.

As for the alleged protest against Paul or Paulinism, this understanding seems to put the cart before the horse. The heart of the
contrast between Paul and James is their different understanding
of Gen. 15:6. However, that is not the *topic* of James 2:14–26 but
only one of several arguments for what James tries to demonstrate.
He begins with the contrast between mere words and useful actions (vv. 14–17); then he confronts the visible deeds with invisible
faith (v. 18); then he ridicules mere faith by attributing it to demons
(v. 19). It is only in a second approach to the problem that Biblical
examples are adduced, at first (vv. 21–24) Abraham according to
Gen. 15:6 and Gen. 22, then Rahab the prostitute according to
Joshua 2:25. The topic of justification (where Paul and James are
at variance) does not turn up in this passage before v. 21. Therefore this difference can hardly be the issue that is at stake in this

---

[12] See e.g., John Calvin, *Institution* III xvii.11–12.
[13] A rare and extreme exception is Martin Hengel, who proposes to read the whole letter
of James as a fierce attack on Paul's theology and character: 'Der Jakobusbrief als an-
tipaulinische Polemik', in *Tradition and Interpretation in the New Testament. Essays in Honor of E.
Earle Ellis*, ed. G. F. Hawthorne and O. Betz (Grand Rapids/Tübingen, 1987), 248–278.

passage. What else is it? We should expect to find it stated clearly at the beginning of the passage. And there it is (v. 14): 'What good is it, my brothers, if a man claims to have faith but has no deeds? Can such faith save him?' This is no attack on Pauline theology at all. Not only because Paul did not teach that which James rejects, but rather because not even the components of the sentence are Pauline! Paul never taught that *faith* (qualified or not) can *save*. Instead, such a phrase is clearly rooted in the synoptic tradition, where Jesus repeatedly says to people whom he has healed: 'Your faith has saved you.'[14] (In Greek, the verb *sozo* is used for healing as well as for saving.) Likewise, the phrase 'to have faith' is attested in the Gospels in the same context of miracle traditions (see Mark 4:40; 11:22; Luke 17:6). It is in this sense that it recurs also in a letter of Paul's (see 1 Cor. 13:2) and in connection with Paul in Acts 14:9. To use this phrase in the context of eschatological salvation is without any precedent in the letters of Paul. Thus, if James is protesting against any teaching that is reflected in v. 14, it is not that of Paul but an overstatement of the importance and impact of faith derived from Jesus traditions of the synoptic type. If we wish to personalise this trajectory, the apostle Paul is certainly no candidate.[15] If compelled to bet or vote, my choice would be – Peter![16]

As for the structure of argument, the case of Romans 4 is different from that in James 2. It is here that Abraham is introduced as the very topic of the passage, and it is Paul who discusses a position he does not share but rejects (that Abraham was justified by works); see Rom. 4:1–2. Moreover, the way in which Paul poses this theoretical possibility (which he regards as unreal) does not from the beginning declare it to be unreal. That is the apostle's style when he comments upon existing opinions of real persons (see 1 Cor. 15:13, 16, 29b, 32c; Gal. 2:21; 3:18; 5:11). Thus, Romans 4 turns out to affirm Paul's view of the Abraham tradition against others who interpret it differently in order to substantiate their teaching on justification. That is why Paul goes on to specify the meaning of Gen. 15:6 by

---

[14] See Matt. 9:22; Mark 5:34; 10:52; Luke 7:50; 8:48; 17:19; 18:42.

[15] See below, ch. 7.

[16] See Acts 3:16; 4:12; 10:43; 15:11 for evidence of faith being emphasised by Peter, and Gal. 2:12 for his being criticised by adherents of James.

discussing the verb *logizomai* with the help of Ps. 32:1–2 (see vv. 4–8) and by recalling the biographical place of Gen 15:6 according to the Biblical narrative (see vv. 9–12). It is clear that Paul is conscious of positions competing with his own and defends his message against appeals to Scripture put forward by (some of) his opponents. If anyone wants to identify the person or position against which Paul is setting his face here, James 2:14–26 makes a meaningful target.

The question how this result relates to the problem of the authorship of the letter attributed to James can for the moment be left open for others to discuss. For the *theology* of Romans 4 it makes no difference whether James 2:14–26 is a later witness, based on tradition, of the position which Paul opposes or the actual voice of James the Just, the brother of Jesus, himself. However, it may be worth mentioning that Gal. 2:11–14 reveals certain tensions between Paul and James (or at least some of his adherents) and that Paul comments upon these tensions by a summary of his teaching on justification (see Gal. 2:15–21), soon followed by a quotation of Gen. 15:6 in Gal. 3:6. It is also worth mentioning that Paul alludes to Ps. 143:2 both in Gal. 2:16 and in Rom. 3:20.

ROMANS AND ACTS

The relationship between the theology of Paul and that of Luke (and between the letters of Paul and the portrait of the apostle in Acts) was a storm-centre of New Testament studies in the first decades after the Second World War.[17] The heat of the debate derived from overtones of the discussion on the level of systematic theology. In the style of the witty saying that *Emil Brunner was playing Melanchthon to Barth's Luther*, it might equally be said that *Luke was held to play Emil Brunner to Paul's Barth*. Since then the theological climate has changed thoroughly and some former verdicts have mutated into compliments. What can be said today about the theology of Romans in comparison with the picture of Paul in Acts?

The easiest way to answer the question whether Luke had a congenial understanding of Paul's theological outlook is to examine the

---

[17] See e.g., Peder Borgen, 'From Paul to Luke', *CBQ* 31 (1969), 168–182; Morton S. Enslin, 'Once Again, Luke and Paul', *ZNW* 61 (1970), 253–271; R. L. Jeske, 'Luke and Paul on the Apostle Paul', *CThM* 4 (1977), 28–38.

speeches which he puts into the mouth of the apostle. To this end, the interest of scholars has been focused on three longer speeches (with their narrative context): the synagogue sermon in Antioch near Pisidia in Acts 13:16–41; the address to the intellectuals of Athens in Acts 17:22–31; and the farewell sermon to the elders of Ephesus in Acts 20:18–35. In addition, we can include observations from the defence speeches in the later chapters of Acts into our reflections.

As for the synagogue sermon, it has never been denied that the climax of this speech in Acts 13:38–39 consciously echoes Paul's teaching on justification:

Therefore, my brothers, I want you to know that through him (sc. Jesus) the forgiveness of sins is proclaimed to you. Through him everyone who believes is justified from everything you could not be justified from by the law of Moses.

However, the actual wording has been criticised as clumsy and betraying only a superficial knowledge of Paul because of the identification of forgiveness and justification, and in view of the 'non-Pauline' construction of 'to justify' with 'from'. What has escaped the attention of these critics is that both phenomena occur in Romans! (See Rom. 4:5–8 and 6:7.) In addition, it is noteworthy that Luke's Paul uses justification language only in this context of a synagogue service – a remarkable parallel with the function of this language in those letters of Paul which contain discussions with, and of, Judaism (Romans, Galatians, and Phil. 3).

Another significant common element of Acts 13 and Romans is the reference to the *promise* given to David as pointing to Jesus, the Son of David (cf. Acts 13:23 with Rom. 1:2–3) and to the *promises* given to the fathers and fulfilled in Jesus (cf. Acts 13:32 with Rom. 15:8). Again, this topic fits excellently into the situation of a synagogue service, and is prominent in Romans and Galatians. Moreover, the quotation of Ps. 2:7 as referring to Jesus as Son of God in Acts 13:32 should not be overlooked because it is paralleled elsewhere in the New Testament. Within Acts it is only Paul who proclaims Jesus as Son of God (here in Acts 13 and in Acts 9:20), a basic idea of Paul's christology, especially in Romans (see Rom. 1:3, 4, 9; 5:10; 8:3, 29, 32; 15:6).

If we include the follow-up conversations after this synagogue sermon in our discussion, we also get an emphasis on grace in Acts 13:43, so typical of Paul in general. Above all, the principle of Rom. 1:16, that the Gospel is addressed to Jews first, is clearly echoed in Acts 13:46 (and illustrated by other reports on Paul's missionary strategy in Acts 14:1; 16:13; 17:1–2, 10, 17; 18:4; 19:8).

Paul's speech on the Areopagus ('Ares Hill') in Athens has been praised and denounced as a model of contextualisation or making use of a 'point of contact'.[18] The controversial issues are Paul's identification of an 'unknown god' venerated by the Athenians with the God whom he proclaims (Acts 17:23), together with the downgrading of pagan polytheism as 'ignorance' in v. 30 and the attempt to introduce the right knowledge of God along philosophical lines and with the help of pagan poets (see vv. 24–29). It is agreed among scholars that Rom. 1:18–23 is the passage in Paul's letters that uses a similar pattern, whether inspired by Wisdom 13–15 or not. But some exegetes have stressed the fact that Paul's verdict in Rom. 1:21 is that 'men are without excuse', while in Acts 17:30 pagan polytheism appears as a pardonable failure: 'In the past God overlooked such ignorance, but now he commands all people everywhere to repent.'

However, the conjunction of 'ignorance' with *repentance* implies an aspect of guilt as does the subsequent warning of God's impending final judgement on mankind in v. 31. On the other hand, in Romans 1:21–22, Paul's verdict on the living generation (as distinct from the original situation of mankind) is 'lack of understanding' and 'foolishness' – to people who pride themselves as 'wise' perhaps more painful than moral lapses! In addition, the notion of a temporary divine forbearance is also attested in Rom. 3:25–26. However, all these caveats are not meant to deny the fact that the Areopagus speech is a singular case in the New Testament – mainly because of its genre as a lecture for intellectuals without the faintest notion of what Paul's message was all about (see Acts 17:18).

[18] See e.g., Martin Dibelius, 'Paul on the Areopagus' and 'Paul in Athens', in his *Studies in the Acts of the Apostles* (London, 1956), 26–92; Bertil Gärtner, *The Areopagus Speech and Natural Revelation* (Uppsala, 1955); Colin J. Hemer, 'The Speeches of Acts, II. The Areopagus Address', *TynB* 40 (1989), 239–259.

As far as genre is concerned, the farewell speech in Acts 20:18–35 offers itself for comparison with the letters of Paul because it is the only speech of Paul in Acts that is addressed to Christians – as are his letters. Moreover, according to the narrative of Acts, it was held during Paul's last journey to Jerusalem, i. e., only weeks after Paul's Letter to the Romans (see Rom. 15:25). The attitude of the apostle in view of this impending visit to Judea is the same in Acts 20:22–24 as in Rom. 15:25, 30–32.

On the other hand, the audience of the speech are fellow-believers who have witnessed Paul's ministry for years (see Acts 20:18–21, 31), while the apostle has not yet been in Rome and knows only some of the addressees of Romans personally. Last but not least, the aspect of farewell is quite the opposite of the purpose of Romans. Thus it is primarily in other letters of Paul (or attributed to Paul) that we must look for passages which resemble Acts 20, and that is not our task here. In any case, the message of Paul as expounded in Romans is well represented in Acts 20:24 by the term 'the gospel of grace' (or God's 'word of grace' in v. 32).

The defence speeches of Paul located in Jerusalem (Acts 22:1–21) and Caesarea (Acts 24:10–21; 26:23–29) breathe the spirit of Romans in that they strongly affirm the Jewish identity of the apostle and his unbroken solidarity with his fellow-Israelites (see Rom. 9:1–3; 10:1; 11:1). Especially his repeated confessions to share the *hope* of Israel (see Acts 23:6; 24:15; 26:6–7 as well as 28:20) are in line with the outcome of Paul's teaching in Romans 9–11.

Perhaps the most striking innovative teaching of Romans 9–11 is Paul's theory of a plan of God behind the Jewish rejection of the Gospel in order to direct the missionary endeavours of the Church towards the Gentiles (see Rom. 11:11–15). This interpretation of the spread of the good news into the Mediterranean world is illustrated by Luke in several narratives (see Acts 8:4; 11:19–21; 13:45–49; 18:5–6; 28:26–28). In most cases this view is stated explicitly in emphatic words addressed to a Jewish audience – perhaps an echo of Paul's hope that the response to the Gospel among Gentiles might provoke at least some Jews to faith (see Rom. 11:14).

Finally, one of the disputed features of Luke's portrait of Paul that is endorsed by the witness of Romans is his role as charismatic miracle-worker: cf. Acts 13:11; 14:8–10; 16:18; 19:11–12 with Rom. 15:19 (and 2 Cor. 12:12).

In an article, 'The Unknown Paul', the Norwegian scholar Jacob Jervell has argued that the letters of Paul do not provide a balanced portrait of the apostle because they are too much influenced by their occasion and purpose under specific circumstances.[19] By contrast, he reckons with oral traditions behind Acts which were less subject to one-sided tendencies. One of his conclusions is that the 'real Paul' of history will have been more Jewish than most of his letters suggest. There is one exception: 'The unfamiliar, unknown Christian Pharisee Paul can be harmonised with only one Pauline letter, with Romans.'[20] Essentially this is a criticism of an ultra-Pauline portrait of Paul that is too much under the spell of Galatians (probably a heritage of Martin Luther's fondness for Galatians). If his conclusion should be accepted by at least a 'mighty minority' of scholars, this could affect the whole paradigm of criteria for evaluating concepts – and whole writings of the New Testament – as Pauline or non-Pauline. For my part, I am ready to second Jervell's motion.

ROMANS AND THE GOSPELS

The obvious lack of Jesus traditions in the letters of Paul (apart from Christ's death and resurrection) has been a challenge to thoughtful interpreters. The only two explicit references to sayings of Jesus are found in 1 Cor. 7:10 (on divorce, see Matt. 5: 31–32 and parallels) and 1 Cor. 9:14 (on financial support for preachers of the Gospel; see Matt. 10:10 and Luke 10:7). In addition, a number of allusions have been identified, some of them in Romans: Rom. 12:14 echoes Jesus's call to love one's enemy (see Matt. 5:43–44), and the words against retaliation in Rom. 12:17–21 are reminiscent of Matt. 5:38–39. Paul's plea for subordination under the ruling powers in Rom. 13:1–7 may be read as an application of Mark 12:13–17 (and parallels), especially since it affirms the duty to pay tributes to the Roman overlords. The warning of the sword in Rom. 13:4 could be inspired by Jesus's word to Peter in Matt. 26:52. Paul's view of

---

[19] See Jacob Jervell, 'The Unknown Paul', in his *The Unknown Paul. Essays on Luke-Acts and Early Christian History* (Minneapolis, 1984), 52–67.

[20] Ibid., my translation from p. 38 of a German version of this paper.

the love command as a summary of all commandments of the Law in Rom. 13:8–10 is only partially in line with the teaching of Jesus because he mentions only the call to love one's neighbour while Jesus had combined the love of God (as Israel's primary duty according to Deut. 6:5) and the love of one's neighbour of Lev. 19:18 (see Mark 12:38–34 parr.).[21]

For quite a long time this picture had been interpreted as resulting from Paul's *theology*. A questionable translation of 2 Cor. 5:16[22] was adduced as proving that in Paul's view the earthly life of Christ, including his teaching, was totally irrelevant. Meanwhile it has been widely acknowledged that the lack of Jesus tradition in most of the letters of the New Testament is a matter of *genre* and not of *theology*.[23] Therefore, the relationship between the theology of Romans and the Jesus tradition of the Gospels is not a matter of quotations but of interpretation. It is the logic of both not the wording that has to be compared.

A promising approach to this question is to start with the fact that both Jesus and Paul had to respond to certain claims of Pharisaism: Jesus because Pharisees criticised him (or his disciples) repeatedly; Paul because he had been brought up as a Pharisee but had changed his mind radically. Both Jesus and Paul witness to the fact that the Pharisees were dedicated to – and (more or less) convinced of – being *righteous* (see Luke 16:15; 18:9; Phil. 3:5–6). Neither Jesus nor Paul denied the fact that some people are more pious and lawabiding than others. What Jesus opposed was the false security and contempt of others that grew out of this earnest endeavour (see Mark 2:13–17 parr.; Luke 15; 18:9–14). Paul learned this lesson in the course or as a consequence of his conversion (see Phil. 3:3, 7–9). Has it influenced his argument in Romans?

The centrality of the topic of righteousness and justification in Romans has been discussed in chapter 4. It has been overlooked by some – and has baffled others[24] – that in Rom. 2:13 Paul makes

---

[21] For reasons which can only be guessed, Paul hesitates to talk of human love of God; the only instances are Rom. 8:28; 1 Cor. 8:3, and (a quotation in) 1 Cor. 2:9.

[22] The phrase *kata sarka* was erroneously taken as an attribute of 'Christ' instead of relating it adverbially to the verbs of knowing.

[23] See C. F. D. Moule, 'Jesus in New Testament Kerygma', in *Verborum Veritas. Festschrift für Gustav Stählin zum 70. Geburtstag*, ed. O. Böcher and K. Haacker (Wuppertal, 1970), 15–26.

[24] See E. P. Sanders, *Paul, the Law, and the Jewish people* (London, 1985), 125–131.

justification dependent on *doing the Law*. To have the Law as part of
the nation's heritage; to listen to the Law in synagogue service; or
even to learn Torah under the guidance of a master is not enough
and not so important as practical observance. That is thoroughly
Pharisaic (and therefore returned on the Pharisees in Matt. 23:2)
and a concern of later Rabbinical teaching. In Romans Paul does
not discard this principle. Rather he pushes it to the extreme and
makes it the standard which all human beings fail to fulfil (see Rom.
2:1; 3:10, 19–20).

A peculiar feature of Paul's teaching on justification in Romans
(as distinct from Galatians) is his reflection on *boasting* as the wrong
attitude in this connection (see Rom. 2:17,23; 3:27; 4:2). It is the
'good feeling' which Paul himself had nourished as a Pharisee,
conscious of his achievements in observing the Law and in actions
that even surpassed the duties of ordinary Israelites (see Phil. 3:6) –
essentially the same feeling that the Pharisee of Luke 18 expresses
in his thanksgiving for what he is and does (see Luke 18:11–12).

In Luke 16:15 Jesus tells the Pharisees that the righteousness
which they profess is only a superficial civic correctness, while their
hearts are detestable in the sight of God. In Rom. 7:7–11 Paul steers
a similar course when he chooses the tenth commandment 'Thou
shalt not covet' as the test-case of what the Law can and cannot
effect in human lives.

In the sequel (Rom. 7:14–25) the apostle defines human sinfulness as weakness (as he had already done in passing in Rom. 5:6),
and this is also the primary meaning of Paul's technical term 'the
flesh'. That is another parallel to the teaching of Jesus in his discussion with Pharisees. When they criticised his being on visiting terms
with 'tax collectors and sinners', he answered with a metaphorical
aphorism: 'It is not the healthy who need a doctor, but the sick
(or, weak). I have not come to call the righteous, but sinners' (Mark
2:17; cf. Matt. 9:12–13; Luke 5:31–32). This is not just a *bon mot*, but
a refusal of a too high esteem of the free will shared by Pharisaic
anthropology. Such an anthropology can easily lead to contempt of
those who have not taken the right decision, while an anthropology
which regards sinners above all as weak and victims of evil powers
promotes compassion. Along this line, Jesus and Paul taught the
importance of making a difference between the *deeds* of sinners and

their *person* – a lesson which the reformers of the sixteenth century repeated and renewed in their doctrine of justification.

A practical outcome of this view of human nature is Jesus's warning not to judge each other (see Matt. 7:1–5), which is echoed in Rom. 2:1 and in the positive exhortation of Rom. 15:7: 'Accept one another, then, just as Christ accepted you'. This final call to solidarity in spite of tensions can be read as a summary of Jesus's answer to the Pharisees in the parable of the prodigal son (see Luke 15:1–2, 12–32), which combines the Gospel of God's loving mercy with a plea for reconciliation in social relations – as does the fifth line of the Lord's prayer (Matt. 6:12; Luke 11:4).

More could be said about the relation between Paul and Jesus on the basis of all of his letters. I hope that the soundings we have taken on the basis of Romans alone have endorsed the thesis of David Wenham, that Paul was not the 'founder of Christianity' but a 'follower of Jesus' – and a very congenial one.[25]

[25] See David Wenham, *Paul. Follower of Jesus or Founder of Christianity?* (Grand Rapids and Cambridge, 1995); also David Wenham, *Paul and Jesus. The True Story* (London: SPCK, 2002).

CHAPTER 8

The impact of Romans and interactions with Romans in Church history

Every modern attempt to delineate the theology of Romans (as of the apostle Paul in general) is indebted to earlier interpretations. It is not only a matter of reading with eyes wide open what the text says, but also the product of a process of evaluation. Our emphasising or downgrading of what we read is not the casual effect of a moment but part of a history of understanding and transmitting the message of the ancient author. Therefore it is a matter of fairness to pay tribute to at least some highlights of the reading of Romans through the centuries. It can also teach us humility and make us ready to accept the shifts of emphasis which the next generation of scholars and expositors will propose as responses to the challenges of their time.

However, one caveat must be mentioned at the beginning. Our notion of a 'theology of Romans' (or of other writings of the New Testament) is a modern concept that did not exist in the minds of ancient or medieval Christian thinkers. Not even the idea of a 'theology of Paul' as distinct from or even in conflict with other 'theologies' of the New Testament had emerged before the rise of historical criticism. It is an offspring of the development in which Biblical studies were emancipated from the tutelage of dogmatic theology; in short, a product of the Enlightenment. In all the centuries before, the interpretation of the Bible had been what an important theological movement of the twentieth century tried to reconstruct: *Biblical theology*. Nevertheless, teachers of the Church with a noteworthy personal profile did have their predilections in their drawing from, and appealing to, Biblical texts. This observation can apply to a single saying or limited passage which became the decisive keyword for a lifelong career (possibly from

Romans). But it can also be true of a whole book of the Bible such as Romans.

THE FIRST LETTER OF CLEMENT

The first question to be asked along this line is whether we know anything about the response of the recipients in Rome to our letter. The only source from the first century AD which we can consult in this matter is 1 Clement, a writing of the Roman church to the sister-church of Corinth. It used to be dated to the nineties of this century (i.e., under Domitian), but recent studies have also considered a date in the seventies. Unfortunately, we have little knowledge of events after AD 70 which affected the Church in a way that could have left traces in Christian literature, and the alleged persecution of Christians under Domitian has been disputed.

As for Paul, it is clear that 1 Clement speaks of him with great respect (see 1 Clem. 5:5–7), with more emphasis (or more biographical knowledge?) than of Peter (see 5:4). The letter contains no *explicit* quotation from Romans which is marked as such by a quotation formula. Instead, it reminds the Corinthians of Paul's first letter to them, especially of its warning of factions in 1 Cor.1 –4 (see 1 Clem. 47). But the concern of this passage and the whole letter is fully in line with the plea for peace and harmony so prominent in Romans.[1] The letter breathes a sheer passion for peace that could be both a sign of the *genius loci* of Rome and a fruit of Paul's congenial interpretation of the Gospel in his Letter to the Romans. On the other hand, it must be conceded that 1 Clement does not reiterate any of the theological arguments of Paul's Letter to the Romans. But for this, various interpretations can be considered. It could mean that (the majority of) the Christians in Rome were not lastingly impressed by the theology of Romans. It could, however, also indicate that Paul's letter had been so convincing that the controversial issues of his time (e.g., the inclusion of Gentiles into the Church without conversion to Judaism and observance of the Law) had been settled meanwhile.

---

[1] See above in chapter 4. For 'peace' in 1 Clem. see 2:2; 3:4; 15:1, 4; 16:5; 19:2; 20:1, 9, 10, 11; 21:1; 22:5; 60:3, 4; 61:1, 2; 62:2; 63:2; 64:1; 65:1 (twice).

JOHN CHRYSOSTOM (C. AD 350–407)

From the eastern part of the ancient Church, John Chrysostom of Antioch and Constantinople has been appraised as 'of monumental importance' for the interpretation of Paul and his letters.[2] In his seven homilies on the apostle, *De laudibus sancti Pauli*,[3] he displays a unique veneration for the apostle. From Paul's Letter to the Romans, it is above all Paul's confession of solidarity with Israel in Rom. 9:3 (culminating in his willingness to pay for it with his eternal salvation!) which is quoted repeatedly with highest respect (see Hom. 1:13, 14; 2:6; 6:2; 7:2). Maybe John's own painful experiences with opponents in Church and state, and his readiness to suffer for his theological convictions, created an identification with Paul in exactly this attitude.

AUGUSTINE (AD 354–430)

In Augustine's biography, a casual reading of Rom. 13:13–14 appears as the decisive incentive for his conversion as described in book VIII of his *Confessions* (§§ 7–12).[4] These exhortations are peripheral in Romans and do not flow out of distinctive features of its theology. Neither is Augustine's response to them a breakthrough on the level of thinking, but rather an act of the will in the context of Augustine's ethical struggles. Accordingly, when he refers to the conversion of Paul, it is not so much its interpretation in Gal. 1 or Phil. 3 that he has in mind, but the ethical interpretation of 1 Tim. 1:15–16, where Paul is the outstanding model of a sinner who meets mercy.[5] His appropriation of the *theology* of Romans has different settings in later contexts of his spiritual development and career as teacher of the Church.[6] It is primarily concerned

---

[2] See Margaret M. Mitchell, *The Heavenly Trumpet. John Chrysostom and the Art of Pauline Interpretation* (Tübingen: Mohr Siebeck, 2000), 5.

[3] Translation into English by Margaret M. Mitchell, *The Heavenly Trumpet*, 440–487.

[4] See G. Bonner, *St Augustine of Hippo. Life and Controversies* (Philadelpha, 1963), 42–52.

[5] See Paula Fredriksen, 'Paul and Augustine: Conversion Narratives, Orthodox Traditions, and the Retrospective Self', *JThSt* 37 (1986), 3–34. Objections against the conclusions of this essays have been raised by F. B. A. Asiedu, 'Paul and Augustine's Retrospective Self: The Relevance of Epistula XXII', *REAug* 47 (2000), 145–164.

[6] See W. Babcock, 'Augustine's Interpretation of Romans (AD 394–396)', *AugSt* 10 (1979), 55–74.

with anthropology and focused on the interpretation of Rom. 7.
It is marked by a radical change of mind resulting from different
challenges he had to face. Initially he had to fight the influence
of Manichaeism, a syncretistic oriental religion which had fascinated him in his youth and which confronted him on his return
from Italy to North Africa around AD 390. This movement tried
to win over converts from Christianity by claiming that the apostle Paul had taught a similar deterministic anthropology. Against
this claim, Augustine emphasised the fact that in Romans 7 the
will is on God's side, and he understood it to be free to choose
between good and evil. But later on, when he was struggling with
Pelagianism, he felt compelled to put the helm over and explicitly
repudiated his earlier exegesis of Rom. 7. He then acknowledged
that 'delight in the law of God' (Rom. 7:22) was much too positive
an attitude to be attributed to natural man.[7] Likewise he could not
accept that Rom. 2:14–16 (on conscience as, possibly, replacing the
Law) was speaking of Gentiles prior to their coming to faith in Jesus
Christ. Thus, Augustine's reception of Romans is a mixture of a
rediscovery of Paul's own theology and a re-reading according to
certain needs felt by a local bishop and respected teacher of the
Church in the struggles of his day.

MARTIN LUTHER (AD 1483–1546)

The same is true of Martin Luther's encounter with the theology of Romans. He had already become a monk (incidentally an
'Augustinian eremit') and a professor of Biblical studies when, in
1515/1516, he had to give lectures on Romans (not published in his
lifetime but discovered and edited in the early twentieth century).
They witness a development in his thinking towards a critical evaluation of scholastic traditions of the late Middle Ages, though not
yet the decisive breakthrough to those truly evangelical convictions
which the Papacy would not tolerate. These were not worked out
in the classroom, but were born from a deep spiritual struggle of
the monk Luther, who despaired of the comfort which the peniten-
tial practice of his Church offered him. According to the doctrine

---

[7] See Fredriksen, 'Paul and Augustine', 22–25.

he had been taught, forgiveness of sins and remittance of punishment in purgatory were dependent on complete confession and
the quality of the penitent's remorse. Luther adopted the radical
position that a remorse that was born merely out of fear of eternal
condemnation (or of temporary punishment in purgatory) was not
enough. Only a deep contrition which implied a real hate of sin
and a genuine love of God and His will was acknowledged as the
basis of forgiveness, and the validity of an absolution after confession was conditioned by this criterion. But who could be quite
sure of the purity of his or her own penitence? Luther had imbibed
too much of Augustine's art of self-critical introspection in order
to trust himself, and without that trust no assurance of forgiveness
could take root in his tormented heart. But then it dawned on him
that the Gospel was not about trusting oneself (one's contrition
or ensuing acts of penitence) but about trusting God and what He
had done for us in Christ, especially in Christ's atoning death at the
cross. He discovered Paul's message of justification by faith alone
without 'works of the Law' as pointing the way out of this crisis.
Having found this comfort, he began to pass it on in his preaching,
using the language of unconditioned absolution for all believers on
the basis of the fully sufficient work of God in Christ. Public controversy began and the reformation of large portions of the Church
was gradually set in motion when Luther attacked the flourishing
trade of letters of indulgence.

Readings in Romans contributed to this development. But it is
well attested that the Letter to the Galatians ranked even higher
in Luther's eyes. He once confessed that he was virtually 'married'
to Galatians. Obviously, he appreciated this letter because it was
more polemical than Romans in style and in content: Luther could
be very impolite in published pamphlets, paying no tribute either
to the social status of his opponents or to his own security.[8] Apart
from that, Galatians was the letter he treated after Romans in AD
1516–1517, and that period is widely held to be the time when his
'evangelical' insight grew most rapidly.

A passage in Romans even seems to have been a hindrance to
his new understanding of the Gospel – and at the same time the

---

[8] See Luther's writing *Contra Henricum regem Angliae* (1522) against King Henry VIII in response to the latter's *Assertio septem sacramentorum adversus Martinum Lutherum* (1521) for which
he was to be honoured by the title *defensor fidei*.

occasion of a deep experience of relief and illumination. It is his famous 'experience in the tower' (possibly a toilet in the cloister of Wittenberg!), which he describes in the preface to the first edition of his collected writings in Latin from AD 1545. There he writes (as an old man more than twenty-five years after the event, he recalls):

I greatly longed to understand Paul's epistle to the Romans and nothing stood in the way but that one expression, 'the justice of God', because I took it to mean that justice whereby God is just and deals justly in punishing the unjust. My situation was that, although an impeccable monk, I stood before God as a sinner troubled in conscience, and I had no confidence that my merit would assuage him. Therefore I did not love a just and angry God, but rather hated and murmured against him. Yet I clung to the dear Paul and had a great yearning to know what he meant. Night and day I pondered until I saw the connection between the justice of God and the statement that 'the just shall live by his faith'. Then I grasped that the justice of God is that righteousness by which through grace and sheer mercy God justifies us through faith. Thereupon I felt myself to be reborn and to have gone through open doors into paradise. The whole Scripture took on a new meaning, and whereas before the 'justice of God' had filled me with hate, now it became to me inexpressibly sweet in greater love. This passage of Paul became to me a gate to heaven . . .[9]

A classical document of Luther's understanding of Romans in his prime is his introduction to Romans in the first edition of his translation of the New Testament (1522). It begins with a praise of Romans as 'the very core of the New Testament and purest gospel which every Christian should not only know by heart word for word (!) and meditate every day . . .'. Then he proceeds to explain the characteristic terms of the theology of the letter: Law (the longest passage), sin, grace and gift, faith, righteousness, flesh and spirit. Then follows an outline of the argument of the letter, where he treats chapters 6–7 at some length, while the passages on chapters 8–16 are remarkably shorter than the average. On the whole, the choice of topics covers the essentials of Romans, apart from the problem of Israel. Instead, chapters 9–11 are mentioned as difficult teaching on providence or predestination. They should be skipped by beginners and are helpful only for those who have thoroughly learned the lessons of chapters 1–8.

---

[9] Translation quoted from Roland H. Bainton, *Here I Stand. A Life of Martin Luther* (London: Hodder and Stoughton, 1951).

A tangible shift of emphasis or modification (in fact a modernisation) of the message of Romans can be observed in Luther's interpretation of the Law. While Paul insisted on the relevance of *doing* as criterion of a person's righteousness, Luther's concern is the inner attitude of the heart. Even perfect observance of the Law (which Luther had claimed for himself just as Paul in Phil. 3:6) is of no value if it is not performed with joy and willingly, not only from fear of punishment in case of transgression. Paul's 'works of the Law' are no longer specific actions which the Law commands (such as circumcision), but all actions which comply with the Law only formally and superficially but do not flow from the innermost feelings of the heart. Exegetically this is a wrong interpretation of Romans, since for Paul the state of the heart is revealed by one's actual behaviour and a possible contrast between 'heart' and 'deed' is restricted to the ritual act of circumcision (see Rom. 2:25–29). Luther's view is closer to sayings of Jesus such as in Matt. 15:1–20 par.; Mark 7:1–23 than to Paul's teaching in Romans. Accordingly, Luther's interpretation of sin in this preface is focused on the heart, so that unbelief turns out to be the essence of sin – a definition borrowed from John 16:8–9, not derived from Romans. (Later, in the passage on righteousness, Rom. 14:23 is quoted as affirmation of this view.)

A jewel of this introduction is the definition of faith as given by God and identical with being born again, so that it cannot but produce good deeds. Without mentioning the letter of James (which Luther did not like), Luther almost literally repeats the warning of James 2 of a faith without deeds. This ethical effect of true faith is confirmed in the passage on Romans 6.

Under the heading 'grace and gift' and in the passage on Rom. 7 we find Luther's application of this chapter to the Christian life as a struggle between flesh and spirit. The wording of the latter passage is coloured by Gal. 5:17 (without quoting it explicitly).

On the whole, Luther's preface shares the original intention of the letter to defend the message of justification by faith against critics, especially by stressing the ethical outcome of true faith.[10]

---

[10] A discussion of John Calvin's preface to his commentary on Romans can be skipped because it is an outline of the argument of the letter that is very close to present interpretations except in sharing Luther's view of Rom. 7.

JOHN WESLEY (AD 1703–1791)

The spiritual biography of John Wesley resembles that of Martin Luther in that he had been a preacher for years before the event which is known as his conversion. The difference between the two is mainly that Wesley even knew the doctrine of justification by faith alone as proclaimed in Romans. But he was more concerned with holiness and progress in sanctification. He also lacked the full assurance of forgiveness in Christ, and conversations with Peter Böhler, a member of the Moravian brethren active in Britain and America, made him doubt whether he really had the faith of which Paul is speaking in Romans. From him Wesley learned that conversion as an event in life which can be dated was the normal beginning of faith both in the New Testament and in later Christian experience. That is what happened to Wesley on 24 May in 1738 in a meeting where Luther's preface to Romans was read. There Wesley found his personal assurance that his sins had been taken away and that he had been released from the law of sin and death.[11] What he had begun to preach even before he experienced it became his emotional possession.

A difference between Luther's reception of Romans and that of John Wesley can be seen in their teaching on sanctification. Luther's interpretation of Romans 7 as describing the inner conflict of believers (*'simul peccator et iustus'*) must have sounded rather pessimistic to Wesley. His conversion was no break with his earlier quest for moral perfection, but was experienced as a breakthrough towards real victory over sin and temptation. That is more in line with Biblical texts such as 2 Cor. 5:17 ('If anyone is in Christ, he is a new creation') and 1 John 5:4 ('Everyone born of God overcomes the world. This is the victory that has overcome the world, even our faith') than with Paul's Letter to the Romans.[12] Tensions between Lutheran Pietism and Methodism (and the Holiness Movement of the late nineteenth century) have their roots in this difference.

---

[11] See *Wesley's Journals* I, 475–476.
[12] While Paul does teach a new ethical quality of the Christian life in Rom. 6:4, 11, to read Rom. 5:10 as teaching a 'victorious life' by the power of the indwelling Christ is against the context of this passage.

KARL BARTH (AD 1886–1968)

In the early twentieth century Paul's Letter to the Romans was instrumental in a different kind of 'conversion' – not of an individual but of large parts of Protestant theology in faculties and in the pulpit. I am speaking of the theological movement initiated by Karl Barth, and especially by his commentary on Romans which appeared in December 1918 (though it bears the number 1919 as the official date of publication). The name of this movement varies, dependent on which allies of Barth are included and on the time envisaged: 'theology of crisis', 'dialectical theology', 'theology of the word of God', 'kerygma theology'. To speak of a conversion can be justified (although Barth was rather sceptical of pietistic evangelism) from Barth's own words. In a letter to his lifelong friend Eduard Thurneysen from the time when the commentary was in the press (11 November 1918), just after the end of the First World War, he wrote: 'If only we had converted to the Bible *earlier* – we would now have firm ground beneath our feet!'

The idea of conversion implies a past that is left behind and looked upon as erroneous and blameworthy. That applies to the theological traditions not of Karl Barth's home (his father had been a Biblical scholar from the 'positive' wing of the reformed church of Switzerland) but to the heritage of liberal theology of the nineteenth century which he had imbibed in his theological education, mainly in Berlin and Marburg. The mainstream of this theology was dominated by philosophical premises from either Kant or Hegel. The primary task of the Church was seen as to cooperate with the leading forces of general culture and to contribute to the moral progress of society. Barth's adherence to this tradition and his respect for his academic teachers was broken when he found their names under a memorandum which endorsed the militarism of Emperor Wilhelm II at the outbreak of the First World War. The increasing barbarism of this war exposed the idea of moral progress as an illusion. Moreover, the whole catastrophe emerged from so-called Christian civilisations which had been regarded as the progressive realisation of the kingdom of God! This moral and spiritual bankruptcy called for a radical revision of the relationship between Church and society as between theology and philosophy. Barth began to listen to the voices of outsiders of the former mainstream, such as Kierkegaard, Dostoevsky, Overbeck, and Blumhardt. But above all he combined his weekly preparations for the sermon in his Swiss parish with digging deep into the Biblical traditions in order to uncover that rock-bottom which would allow a reconstruction of the house of theology on a firm foundation (see Luke 6:48).

The fruits of this re-orientation appeared to the public in Barth's commentary on Romans. Commentary? It was not the type of book to consult for all kinds of historical information and semantic clarification which we expect of a scholarly piece of this literary genre (although it contained good ideas on that level, too). The Dutch theologian A. D. R. Polman has characterised it to the point:

Whoever looks for a careful exposition of a particular text is nearly always disappointed and irritated because the work is with exceptions a construction of Barth rather than an exposition of Paul. Ideas are expanded and embellished which never occurred to Paul, and yet our interest remains undiminished. Because of the style, the content, and the vigorous and passionate convictions which accompany every sentence, the reader is fascinated, and wounded to the heart[13]

Viewed from the distance of several decades, the book can be classified among the literary productions of expressionism, both for its style and its content. Thus, strangely enough, Barth's fierce farewell to any synthesis of theology and secular culture shows clear signs of sharing general trends of European civilisation after the shock of the First World War. This is also why the book was greeted with enthusiasm and triggered a theological revolution in those years of political unrest and upheaval.

It is not easy to give a short survey of the wide discharge of challenges contained in the book. By no means every later development of Barth's theology is anticipated in his 'Romans'. In fact, it underwent a thorough revision for the second edition in 1922. If we restrict ourselves to those points that are of special importance in comparison with Paul's theology in Romans, several aspects may be remarkable.

---

[13] See A. D. R. Polman, *Barth*, trans. Calvin D. Freeman (Nutley, N.J.: Presbyterian and Reformed Publishing Co., 1977), 11.

The most fundamental shift of emphasis is that Barth is concentrating on theology proper while the issues of Romans are mainly soteriological (the necessity and the scope of salvation for Jews and Gentiles) and ethical (sanctification as the necessary and 'natural' outcome of identification with Christ's death and resurrection). Barth's primary message is that God is the 'completely other' different from all human ideas of the divine, either philosophical or religious. In other words, he insists on the necessity (and historical reality) of a revelation of God as a vertical movement from above with no preparation or contribution from the human side. Moreover, all attempts to construct or to mediate aspects of this revelation by intellectual or emotional endeavours not only fail but go astray and lead away from the true revelation of God which is attested in Scripture and which occurs again and again when and where it pleases the Spirit.

No doubt, the Letter to the Romans does contain statements which point in this direction: that the righteousness of God had to be, and has been, revealed in the mission of Christ (see Rom. 3:21) and is hidden to those who oppose that revelation (see Rom. 10:2–4); that the future of Israel is a mystery which had to be disclosed through the apostle (see Rom. 11:25); and that the end of history will vindicate a hitherto hidden harmony between the conflicting ways of God with Israel and with the nations, a conviction that calls for a praise of God's wisdom which surpasses all human understanding (see Rom. 11:30–34).[14] But the radicalism of Barth's opposition to all cultural achievements and religious expectations sounds more like an echo of 1 Cor. 1:18–31 than of Romans. Still, the idea of the Gospel as a stumbling-block to the Jews (1 Cor. 1:23) recurs in Rom. 9:32–33 and gives Barth the opportunity to ground his critique of human religion in this letter of Paul.

The price he paid for this actualisation of the message of Romans, for its application to the crisis of liberal theology and bourgeois Christianity, was that Israel ceased to be the *theme* of large parts

---

[14] The doxology of Rom. 16:25–27 speaks also of 'the revelation of the mystery hidden for long ages past, but now revealed and made known . . .'. In the first edition of his commentary, Barth had presupposed the authenticity of these verses, but in the second edition of 1922 he sided with those exegetes who regarded them as a later addition (the majority view of today).

of Paul's argument in Romans. Instead, Judaism and the 'works of the Law' figure as *models* of the vain confidence of religious people (including Christians!) who claim to know God and to have him on their side.[15] In the second edition of Barth's commentary, the passage Rom. 9:30–10:3 runs under the heading 'Die Schuld der Kirche' ('The Guilt of the Church'), and even the question whether there is a distinctive dignity of the Jews (Rom. 3:1) is discussed in a way which makes the Jews a mere metaphor for all kinds of people with a sense of moral superiority.

It must be added that in the course of time and in response to the triumph of antisemitism in Germany and in countries under German domination, Karl Barth became more sensitive to the abiding covenant of God with his chosen people,[16] and among his pupils are many pioneers of the world-wide rediscovery of Israel in Christian theology.

[15] German soldiers of the First World War bore the inscription 'God with us' on the buckles. Is the message of 'In God we trust' much better?

[16] For a later exposition of Romans 9–11 by Karl Barth, see his *Church Dogmatics*, vol. II:2 (1942), § 34. A shorter commentary on Romans by Karl Barth, *Kurze Erklärung des Römerbriefes* (based on lectures for the general public) appeared in 1956 (Munich: Chr. Kaiser Verlag).

CHAPTER 9

The relevance of Romans reconsidered

In this concluding chapter I am going to point out aspects of the theology of Romans which I regard as important contributions to present-day developments in theology, or as promising answers to challenges felt to be urgent in our time. Perhaps I should apologise for straining the term 'present-day' too much when I include developments that emerged thirty or forty years ago. It is not only because I hesitate to treat my own lifetime as a chapter of past history, but also because I have the impression (and hope) that these developments will keep going and continue to bear fruits in the near future.

ROMANS AND THE RECONCILIATION BETWEEN CHRISTIANS AND JEWS

In the years after the Second World War the horrors of the holocaust were recognised as a challenge to traditional Christian theology. It was conceded that the organised crimes against the Jewish people were the product of a racism that was hostile not only to the Jews but also to most of the genuinely Christian traditions. Nevertheless, it had to be admitted that a traditional anti-Judaism among Church members had paved the way for Hitler's rise to power, and had produced a fatal indifference towards the increasing sufferings of Jews in Germany and in other European countries which were occupied by Germans during the war. The conclusion was inevitable that traditional Christian education and the theological teaching behind it had to be taken to task for this failure. The problem was not only that quite a number of theologians, including some New Testament scholars, had been actively involved in anti-Jewish propaganda. Much more disturbing was the growing awareness of anti-Jewish potential implied in time-honoured concepts of theology and even piety such as the understanding of the Church as the 'new' or 'true' Israel that had replaced the original or historical people of the covenant. (The Jews in turn were held to have been 'disinherited' by God because of their failure to accept the earthly mission of Jesus and the preaching of the apostles.)

As for the role of the New Testament in this context, controversies arose between those who did not hesitate to trace anti-Judaism back to the New Testament itself (e.g., to the passion narratives of the Gospels)[1] and those who preferred to lay the blame on unthoughtful later interpretations. While there is no evidence to justify the assumption that violent hostility towards the Jewish people was intended by any writing of the New Testament, it cannot be denied that bitter feelings against, and harsh verdicts upon (the majority of contemporary) Jews are attested in a number of passages. However, a 'hermeneutic of suspicion' has often gone too far in assuming distortions of historical facts dictated by anti-Jewish tendencies. In some cases the traditions of Bible translation have exacerbated New Testament statements concerning the Jews which are less polemical when translated more exactly.[2] As far as Paul's Letter to the Romans is concerned, the chapters on Israel's failure and future clearly contributed much to the re-orientation of Christian theology in many countries. Especially the metaphor of the olive tree in Rom. 11:17–24 spoke to the hearts of many people. As a result, a number of churches in European countries and in North America (both Protestant and Roman Catholic) issued solemn declarations confessing their collective share of responsibility for the holocaust, promising to revise their teaching and amending their church orders.

However, it must be kept in mind that this process as yet has been more or less restricted to Western European and North American

---

[1] See e.g., Rosemary Ruether, *Faith and Fratricide. The Theological Roots of Anti-Semitism* (New York: Seabury Press, 1974), ch. 2.

[2] E.g., the Greek text of Matt. 27:25 is no wish or curse (nor is the close parallel in Acts 18:6). In Rom. 2:17 the beginning of the verse with 'if' had disappeared in some of the manuscripts and was neglected by many translations so that the whole passage was no longer a theoretical case but a denunciation of 'the' Jew in general.

countries. That is, a positive attitude towards the Jewish people has not yet gained ground in large sectors of the ecumenical movement, neither in the orthodox churches of Eastern Europe nor in the former 'Third World' countries of Africa, Asia, and South America. Lack of solid information on the Near Eastern conflict and the difficulty of distinguishing between the present state of Israel and the historical people of Israel through the centuries produce additional barriers to accepting the message of Romans 9–11. Last but not least, Paul's idea of God's guidance behind Israel's refusal of the Gospel must be hard to swallow for churches that were founded by missionaries who emphasised the importance of personal decision for faith in Christ as the basis of salvation. Thus, the theology of Romans remains a lesson to be learned for many individual Christians and for whole churches in the century that has dawned upon us. It is a theology that urges us to endure the tensions between the logic of the Gospel of salvation in Christ alone, on the one hand, and the promises of God to the patriarchs and their descendants, the historical, empirical people of Israel, on the other. If the mission of Jesus, the Jew, was primarily to the Jews and to make good those promises (see Rom. 15:8), then we have no right to abandon our hope for Israel and our solidarity with Israel. This attitude does not rule out sorrow and anxiety over failures of Jewish people (or their leaders); on the contrary, it even demands such feelings (see Rom. 9:3). Justification as proclaimed in the Letter to the Romans is for sinners, not for sins, and sin is a menace to all human life, including Jews (see Rom. 6:23; 2:9). But that is neither God's first word nor His last concerning Israel (see Rom. 11:25–27).

ROMANS AND THE REFORMATION: THE LIMITS AND THE LEGACY OF LUTHER

In Western Europe, the great day of the apostle Paul and especially of his Letter to the Romans was certainly the sixteenth century. 'Justification in Christ by grace and faith alone' became the hallmark of large church bodies whose theological convictions forced them into independence from the Papacy. Paradoxically, the attribute 'Roman' (in connection with 'catholic') was vested with connotations that stand in contrast with the 'Roman' interpretation of the Gospel in the New Testament. Meanwhile, times have changed thoroughly. The Roman Catholic church of today has left far behind some positions which Luther and other reformers had criticised (while producing other peculiarities that perpetuate the schism of Christianity, such as the dogmas of papal infallibility or of the assumption of the Virgin Mary into heaven). Catholic scholars have produced commentaries on Romans which display not only great knowledge but also deep sympathy for the theology of this letter.[3]

By contrast, the congeniality between Martin Luther and the apostle Paul has been questioned thoroughly by Protestant scholars, one of whom (Krister Stendahl) even served as Lutheran bishop of Stockholm for some time.[4] They deplore Luther's lack of awareness of the ecumenical perspective of Romans and of the missionary drive behind this letter. No doubt, by the time of Martin Luther Christians had, as a rule, lost sight of most of the controversies of Early Christianity. While Paul had to defend the equal standing of Gentile Christians together with Jewish believers, converts from Judaism had become a rare exception among Church members. In fact, the very idea of 'conversion from Judaism to Christianity' is an anachronism when applied to the first century, because in those days neither Paul nor any other Christian of Jewish origin ceased to be a Jew when coming to faith in Christ. Apart from many other indicators, Paul's frequent appeal to the Holy Scriptures – in Romans from the very start (see Rom. 1:2) – proves that the idea of a new religion named Christianity was completely beyond his horizon. On the other hand, he emphatically denied the necessity for Gentile believers to become Jews and to adopt the Jewish way of life. That is what he had to defend against more conservative Jewish Christians in his letters to the Galatians and to the Romans. His various teachings about the Law are essentially an apology of this missionary policy. By contrast, Martin Luther had boldly applied Paul's argument against the 'Judaists' to problems of late medieval piety and Church discipline.

[3] See e.g., the commentaries of Joseph A. Fitzmyer or Brendan Byrne in the suggestions for further reading below.
[4] See Krister Stendahl, *Paul Among Jews and Gentiles and Other Essays* (Philadelphia: Fortress Press, 1976).

The 'new perspective' on the apostle Paul which – as far as the English-speaking world is concerned – was inaugurated by Krister Stendahl, Ed P. Sanders, and James D. G. Dunn in the last quarter of the twentieth century is essentially a rediscovery or revaluation of the *pragmatics* of Paul's theology, especially in Galatians and Romans, which had been neglected by an all too dogmatic or (in theory) 'timeless' reading of these letters.[5] In addition, these studies corrected a fatal consequence of Luther's 'merging of horizons': his application of Paul's polemics against radical Jews to the official teaching and policy of the Papacy produced a distorted picture of Judaism which gradually spread in the minds of Protestant Christians and helped to depreciate the Jews in the eyes of the public. A closer reading of ancient Jewish sources revealed that Paul's emphasis on God's grace and mercy was by no means contrary to Jewish convictions. Thus, recent scholarship on Paul has cautioned us against some *shadows* of the powerful reception of Romans in the European Reformation of the sixteenth century and (probably more so) in Protestant theology of the following centuries.

However, this sensibility to differences between the original intentions of Pauline theology and Luther's application of his teaching to questions of a later age should not create a feeling of superiority on our side. We must keep in mind that our deeper understanding of Judaism is, to a large extent, the result of our knowledge of ancient Jewish sources which were discovered, or made accessible to a wider public, during the twentieth century. In addition, our readiness to read Jewish sources with empathy is a fruit of the lessons of history on the tragic consequences of anti-Judaism. And, finally, the question is whether our interpretation of Paul's letters creates a sense of relevance for today which can bear comparison with Luther's achievement in his day.

In any case, the *content* of Paul's Letter to the Romans itself is more than a mirror of his *intentions*. It is itself the result of an *encounter* between a whole world of traditions and convictions present in Paul's

<hr>

5 For studies in German which prepared the way for this development, see Stephen Westerholm, *Israel's Law and the Church's Faith. Paul and his Recent Interpreters* (Grand Rapids: Eerdmans, 1988), chs. 2 and 3, on William Wrede, Albert Schweitzer, and Hans Joachim Schoeps.

mind and the challenges of his situation and that of the addressees in their Roman environment.[6] The very fact of varying applications of New Testament writings in the course of their interpretation witnesses to this *surplus of semantics over pragmatics*. A writing like Paul's Letter to the Romans contains messages that go far beyond what Paul wanted to tell the Romans at the moment of its composition. His initial self-designation as apostle and servant is no mere claim to authority. It points to his being more of a channel than an author of what he has to convey. In a way that applies more or less to literature as such. But it is all the more true of an author who explicitly subscribes to this truth. That opens the way to discover meanings of what Paul wrote in contexts he could not have dreamed of. Criticism of Luther's exposition and application of Paul must be balanced by attempts to relate the message of Romans to challenges of our time and to forebodings of a future which our children might have to face.

A telling example of continuity and transformation may be seen in the perception of sin in Luther's exegesis of Romans, and in the experience of millions during the twentieth century. Luther confesses to have lived a blameless life as a monk, but discovered sin by investigating the innermost motivations of his heart. Paul's message of justification spoke to the torments which this introspective trial had produced. The twentieth century has experienced the triumph of sin in universal bloodshed and suppression in many countries. The contemporary challenge of sin is not so much the feeling of guilt in individuals which cries for forgiveness, but the power of sin in global dimensions which cries out to be broken. But in both contexts the message of the Gospel as attested by Paul's Letter to the Romans is about God's passionate 'No' to the destructive forces of sin, and His equally passionate love for all human beings, His creatures, beloved in spite of their being involved in the manifold manifestations of evil. While Luther found his comfort above all in Romans 3:21–26, a contemporary application of the theology of Romans may perhaps concentrate on Rom. 1:18–32 and Rom. 8:18–39. But that is just a suggestion for further discussion, the

---

[6] See James D. G. Dunn, *The Theology of Paul the Apostle* (Edinburgh: Clark, 1998), § 25:1: Paul's theology as dialogue.

outcome of which depends on one's place in current conditions
and developments.

THE ABIDING MESSAGE OF ROMANS FOR
A DISILLUSIONED WORLD

The following reflections are rather tentative because they come
from a continental European author writing for students, colleagues, and parts of the general public in the English-speaking
world. On critical examination, my perspective of world affairs
and the 'human condition' may even turn out typically German,
a product of the trials and tensions of the twentieth century in a
country torn by conflicting ideologies and powers, having lived under the 'shield' (and shadow!) of atomic weapons for many years.
Future historians will perhaps date the end of this era a decade
earlier than the end of the century – with the collapse of the socialist empire and the beginning of military confrontations between
Western powers and Islamic countries. But this perspective, if seen
from a distance, may one day turn out much too 'Northern' and
limited to military history. The real challenges of the future may
emerge in the fields of economy – not so much monetary economy
but economy of natural resources – or health. Already now certain diseases menace not only millions of individuals but the vital
structures of whole societies in Africa and, increasingly, in Eastern
Europe.

Meanwhile, the end of the ideological confrontation between
East and West has created a vacuum of values which used to hold societies together and created solidarity within groups of nations. The
relative stability of two conflicting 'Worlds' with a 'Third World'
trying to profit from the tensions between the other two has been
replaced by a globalisation that is miles away from what deserves
to be called a 'new world order'. While socialist systems have col-
lapsed in most countries, socialist theories on capitalism may come
true with no promise to mend the harm. The secular globalisation
which we are experiencing now is not a movement towards the
unity of mankind in harmony, but only to the increasing breaking
down of barriers to commercial competition. National boundaries
lose many of their former functions, so that governments in turn

lose their influence on many aspects of the life of their citizens. Eventually the idea of national independence and democracy as 'government of the people and by the people' may become an empty concept.

At the same time, and in part as a result of, or reaction to this globalisation, people prefer to define their social identity in terms of smaller ethnic groups or (regional or international) religious communities. The consequences are separatist wars such as in former Yugoslavia and the growth of fundamentalism in societies which have no share in the benefits (and profit) of the global market. One of the roots of political radicalism (and of its worst fruit, terrorism) is the obvious melting down of the great idea of liberty from a comprehensive human right to mere economic liberalism as the dominant force of political reality. Likewise, the idea of progress has come true on the level of science and technology, but not in the sphere of human relations, both individually and globally. Thus, the whole heritage of the Enlightenment has been brought into discredit and religious alternatives have gained new plausibility. Unfortunately, the less peaceful ones turn out more attractive for those who pay the price for growing wealth and welfare in other parts of the world.

With this outlook in mind, I read the Letter to the Romans with its emphasis on peace and justice as a manifesto of an alternative 'globalisation' and as a new vision of 'united nations' – united in the spirit of the kingdom to come which is 'righteousness, peace and joy' (see 14:17) and in the unanimous praise of God in many tongues (see 15:7–13). By contrast, Paul's diagnosis of the present state of humankind (see 3:17: 'They do not know the way of peace') can no longer be dismissed as undue pessimism. Even his deeper analysis of human affairs in Rom. 1:18–32 demands to be considered seriously by all who share a concern for the future of the world: could it not be simply *true* that human existence loses its balance when our thankful admiration of God, the source of all life, is tending towards nil while all our energies are focused on, and spent for, material values or sensations which soon fade away? That disorder and distress in human relations are a consequence of our losing that ethical orientation which flows out of gratitude for God's gifts and attention to His instructions for using them reasonably?

Again, there is Paul's view that none of us is the inventor of his or her moral failure, but all of us are born into traditions which contain the seeds of moral failure, simply because our parents, teachers, and other models of behaviour shape our thinking and conduct not only with their virtues but also with their vices (see Rom. 5:12–14). Is that not more convincing than holding every individual fully responsible for the failures of his or her life? And what about Romans 7? The fascination of the forbidden could not be proverbial if the phenomenon were not common. Though few of us would like to label ourselves as practically obsessed by an evil spirit named 'Sin' (Paul's alternative to being indwelled and guided by the Spirit of God), must we not subscribe to his confession of acting against our inmost convictions or better knowledge (time and again or habitually, in smaller or larger areas of our life)?

It is especially this chapter of Paul's anthropology which anticipates the breakdown of ethical idealism which the twentieth century has produced or revealed. If there is any lesson which this century demands to learn, then it is the lesson on the failure of high moral standards, though accepted almost universally, to check irrational sources of conflict such as the reckless pursuit of wealth, power, or glory which led the nations of Europe into the First World War. The decades that followed witnessed the corruption of lofty ideals themselves in ideologies which abused well-sounding words (whether conservative, as in Nazi propaganda, or revolutionary, as in socialist propaganda) in order to establish ruthless regimes and to gain the consent of the masses for incredible crimes.

With these memories in mind, the message of Romans is relevant not only because it proclaims a different set of moral standards, such as peace and justice and tolerance, but rather because it offers a deeper foundation of ethics and stronger motivations for putting good principles into practice. In essence, the ethics of Romans rest on, and flow from, our gratitude for what God has done for us in Christ (see 12:1: 'Therefore, I urge you *in view of God's mercy . . .*'). In an unprecedented move against the powers of evil, God has paid the price for all human failure in Christ's death, revealing and at the same time exhausting the destructiveness of sin (see 3:24–26; 5:6–11). After this battle, documented to have been victorious by Christ's resurrection, it would be anachronistic to stay under the spell of evil instead of responding gladly to God's love for us in serving Him (see Rom. 6). With this response, human existence is restored to its commission to use, preserve, and enjoy the world entrusted to us, but to praise God, now not only as our Creator but also as our Saviour.

This message contains neither the promise nor the order 'to make the world Christian'. Salvation in the full sense of the word is a matter of the future and of God's own final intervention (see 8:24; 13:11). Nevertheless, the anticipation of this aim of history and the assurance of its realisation are so overwhelming that faith in Christ can produce high spirits amidst very uncongenial circumstances (see 5:1–5; 8:18, 28–39). Thus, in an age of growing anxiety, the message of Romans is a word of comfort and a call to take courage.

Further reading

INTRODUCTIONS

Morgan, R. *Romans* (New Testament Guides), Sheffield Academic Press, 1995

Wedderburn, A. J. M. *The Reasons for Romans*, Edinburgh: T. & T. Clark, 1988, Paperback, 1991

COMMENTARIES OF ROMANS

Barrett, C. K. *A Commentary on the Epistle to the Romans*, London: Black, 1962, repr. 1984

Bruce, F. F. *The Letter of Paul to the Romans. An Introduction and Commentary* (*TNTC*), Leicester Grand Rapids, 1985

Byrne, B. *Romans* (Sacra Pagina Series 6), Collegeville, Minn., 1996

Cranfield, C. E. B. *A Critical and Exegetical Commentary on the Epistle to the Romans* (ICC), Vol. I: Introduction and Commentary on Romans I–VIII, Edinburgh 1975, repr. with corrections 1985, Vol. II: Commentary on Romans IX–XVI and Essays, Edinburgh, 1979, repr. 1983 (with corrections) abridged version: *Romans. A Shorter Commentary*. Grand Rapids: Eerdmans, 1985

Dunn, J. D. G. (ed.) *The Cambridge Companion to St Paul*, Cambridge: Cambridge University Press, 2003.
   Romans 1–8. Romans 9–16 (Word Biblical Commentary 38 A/B), 2 vols., Dallas, 1988

Fitzmyer, J. A. *Romans. A New Translation with Introduction and Commentary*, AncB 33, London, 1993

Haacker, K. *Der Brief des Paulus an die Römer* (ThHK 6), Leipzig: Evangelische Verlagsanstalt, 1999, repr. 2002

Moo, D. J. *The Epistle to the Romans*, NIC, Grand Rapids, 1996

Morris, L. *The Epistle to the Romans*, Grand Rapids/Leicester, 1988

Ziesler, J. *Paul's Letter to the Romans*, London/Valley Forge, 1989, repr. 1993

SPECIAL STUDIES

Barrett, C. K. *Paul. An Introduction to His Thought*, London, 1994
Bassler, J. M. *Divine Impartiality. Paul and a Theological Axiom*, Chico: Scholars Press, 1982
Bruce, F. F. *Paul, Apostle of the Free Spirit*, London, 1977
Campbell, W. S. *Paul's Gospel in an Intercultural Context. Jew and Gentile in the Letter to the Romans*, Frankfurt Bern New York Paris, 1991
Donfried, K. P. *The Romans Debate*, rev. and exp. edn, Peabody: Hendrickson, 1991
Dunn, J. D. G. *The Theology of Paul the Apostle*, Edinburgh: T. & T. Clark, 1998
Elliott, N. *The Rhetoric of Romans. Argumentative Constraint and Strategy and Paul's Dialogue with Judaism*, Sheffield: JSOT Press, 1990
Garlington, D. *Faith, Obendience, and Perseverance. Aspects of Paul's Letter to the Romans*, Tübingen: Mohr Siebeck, 1994
Guerra, A. J. *Romans and the Apologetic Tradition. The Purpose, Genre and Audience of Paul's Letter*, SNTS Mon. Ser. 81, Cambridge, 1995
Haacker, K. 'Paul's Life', in J. D. G. Dunn (ed.), *The Cambridge Companion to St Paul*, Cambridge: Cambridge University Press, 2003, pp. 19–33.
Hay, D. M. and Johnson, E. E. (eds.) *Pauline Theology, Vol. III Romans*, Minneapolis: Fortress, 1995
Horsley, R. A. (ed.) *Paul and Empire. Religion and Power in Roman Imperial Society*, Harrisburgh: Trinity, 1997
Jervis, L. A. *The Purpose of Romans. A Comparative Letter Structure Investigation*, Sheffield: JSOT, 1991
Longenecker, R. N. *Paul, Apostle of Liberty. The Origin and Nature of Paul's Christianity*, Grand Rapids, 1977
Longenecker, Richard N. (ed.) *The Road from Damascus. The Impact of Paul's Conversion on His Life, Thought, and Ministry*, Grand Rapids/Cambridge: Eerdmans, 1997
Minear, P. S. *The Obedience of Faith. The Purposes of Paul in the Epistle to the Romans*, London, 1971
Räisänen, Heikki, *Paul and the Law* (WUNT 29), Tübingen: Mohr Siebeck, 1983
Sanders, E. P. *Paul and Palestinian Judaism. A Comparison of Patterns of Religion*, London: SCM, 1977
   Paul, the Law, and the Jewish People, London: SCM, 1985
Stendahl, K. *Final Account. Paul's Letter to the Romans*, Minneapolis: Fortress, 1995

Stowers, S. K. *Letter Writing in Greco-Roman Antiquity*, Philadelphia: Westminster Press, 1986

Walters, J. C. *Ethnic Issues in Paul's Letter to the Romans. Changing Self-Definitions in Earliest Roman Christianity*, Valley Forge, Penn., 1993

Watson, F. *Paul, Judaism and the Gentiles. A Sociological Approach*, SNTS Mon. Ser. 56, Cambridge: Cambridge University Press, 1986

Wenham, D. *Paul. Follower of Jesus or Founder of Christianity?* Grand Rapids/Cambridge: Eerdmans, 1995

Westerholm, S. *Israel's Law and the Church's Faith. Paul and His Recent Interpreters*, Grand Rapids: Eerdmans, 1988

Index of authors

References

Index of subjects

Includes persons referred to but not names of authors.